D1608331

Ernst Neizvestny.

Ernst Neizvestny.

Life and Work

By Erik Egeland

 **MOSAIC PRESS**
OAKVILLE NEW YORK LONDON

World copyright © 1984 Aventura Forlag
Arbiensgt. 7, 0253 Oslo 2, Norway

English Language Edition   ©   1984 Mosaic Press

Published by Mosaic Press, P.O. Box 1032, Oakville, Ontario L6J 5E9, Canada

In Canada: Mosaic Press, P.O. Box 1032, Oakville, Ontario L6J 5E9
In the United States: Flatiron Books, 175 Fifth Avenue, Suite 814, New York, N.Y. 10010, U.S.A.
In the U.K.: John Calder (Publishers) Ltd, 18 Brewer Street, London, W1R 4AS, England
In New Zealand: Pilgrims South Press, P.O. Box 5101, Dunedin, New Zealand
In Australia: Book Wise International, 1 Jeanes street, Beverly, 5009, South Australia, Australia

ISBN 0-88962-276-0

Set in Baskerville 12 pt, printed on Kymart 150 g.
and bound by Werner Söderström Oy, Finland 1984.

Translated from the Norwegian by John Poole

Photographers:
   Tapio Airaksinen
   Nina Alovert
   Sverre Bergli
   Ulf Johansson
   John Kasparian
   Victor Macarol
   Jean Mohr

One hundred copies of this book are numbered in two series from 1–50.
Included with each book is a set of 4 original etchings by Ernst Neizvestny,
a different set for each series, limited to 50 copies. Each etching is
numbered and signed by the artist. The books are bound in half leather with
gilt edging.

Contents

Author's Note

I am greatly indebted to Ernst Neizvestny himself for wanting me to write this book. I shall never forget his unselfish and inspiring helpfulness. Without this, there could have been no book.

Many kind thoughts go to Leif Hovelsen who encouraged me to undertake this project, and to Milla Braigen and Alex Milits, the two interpreters who worked selflessly for hours on end making it possible for Ernst Neizvestny to use his native language in imparting to me his wealth of ideas and thoughts.

I would also like to thank all those who, both officially and unofficially, enabled me to obtain a first-hand impression of life in the Soviet art world during my two visits to Moscow.

The British writer and art critic John Berger, wrote a book at the end of the nineteen sixties entitled "*Art and Revolution*" about Ernst Neizvestny's art and his position in the Soviet art world, and this has naturally had an influence on the present work. There would indeed have been no point in producing yet another book on this subject unless other relevant aspects of Neizvestny's life and art had come to light supplementing the very penetrating observations and interpretations upon which Berger's work is based. Such aspects have been uncovered, supported by a wealth of new material.

My most important motive for taking it upon myself to write this book is to be found in what I, rightly or wrongly, see as something essentially Russian in the subject matter. Mankind's need for a universal conception of the world and those who live in it is here at the forefront, as is its need to see itself as a branch of the Tree of Life, to borrow the imagery of Neizvestny's central work. This striving towards synthesis, with its origins in spiritualistic experiences and contemplation, runs through the whole of Ernst Neizvestny's strongly differentiated production. It seems to me that this is something of particular relevance to the pluralistic art circles of the Western world, trying as they are to position themselves among amputated philosophical and psychological concepts.

Oslo, September 1984

Erik Egeland

Photo collage of the "Tree of Life", the ultimate objective of all Ernst Neizvestny's artistic production. The artist envisions a structure rising some three hundred feet above ground level and going down sixty feet below. Its whole conception and form language are such that Neizvestny is certain that it had no chance of being commissioned in the Soviet Union. His hopes rest on the USA.

The "Tree of Life"

Having finally extricated himself from the Soviet Union, Ernst Neizvestny has issued a challenge to both East and West. His life has long been dominated by a vision of a single all-embracing work of art in which Mankind's contradictory facets are assembled; a project upon which he has been working for more than a quarter of a century. He has built a scale model, he has completed numerous of its sculptured constituent parts. He has filled seven albums with long series of detailed drawings in black and white, illustrating the intricacies of its design; a monumental composition which he once called the "Heart of Man". Nowadays he refers to it as the "Tree of Life" and claims that he is all set to realise the project, only lacking a site and the necessary funds. Building it will be no problem he says, since he has long since perfected the special construction methods he intends to use.

"This work is a task that I have set myself; I want to try and create a new entirety such as can be found in the ancient temples. A multiplexity of sculpture and light, of painting and ritual."

Whether his challenge is artistically acceptable is a matter for each and every one of us to judge for himself. Interestingly, such judgements are being made at the present time and have given rise to debate. But there is no doubt at all that Neizvestny's purpose, his striving towards universality, is a rare phenomenon in the world of art today.

An extra dimension is provided by his personal experiences fighting in the front line of the struggle for artistic freedom; a dramatic testimony on the fate of creative artists in our time.

In the Soviet Union he had to work on the "Tree of Life" under ground with no hope of ever seeing the project realised under the existing régime. His position, described by Harrison E. Salisbury, as "the best known, wealthiest and most contro-versial artist in the Soviet Union" had nothing to do with this vast project of his. His reputation was founded upon other monumental works and most of all upon the sculptures and etchings which he exhibited as individual works of art. Many of these however, were in fact created as components of the "Tree of Life".

In 1976 he coerced the Soviet authorities into giving him permission to emigrate to Western Europe. He left Europe for the United States in 1977 and it is on the North American continent that he hopes to plant his "Tree of Life", a project which would boast dimensions the like of which the world has never seen.

The idea behind the tree is at variance with his native country's totalitarian view of Man, Society and History. Furthermore it relegates the western world's materialism and cult of the rational to a secondary role. He sees our conflicting philosophies, our funds of specialised knowledge and our schools of thought as being encompassed within a single universe, a living entirety full of both meaning and mystery. His vision of totality is at once all-embracing and open, free from proselytizing ideologies.

Undaunted he stands up for the concept of synthesis in our pluralistic cultural environment. He is a child of our scientific and restlessly technological age and the complex nature of his mode of artistic expression comfirms this. But he faces up to the present with what amounts to a sense of timelessness. He is clearly conscious of the closeness of his links with past epochs, peoples and works of art. Ancient Egypt, Mexico and Greece, the Middle Ages in Europe, Dante, Dostoyevsky and Michel-angelo are all important to him. His art bears witness to this.

He comes from a people, from a country, that had no Renaissance period in its history. Nevertheless, he understands, though he does not accept, the dividing lines between religion, art and science.

It would be futile to try and put Ernst Neizvestny's personal philosophy into words.

Bronze of the "Tree of Life"
Modelled in 1969 and cast in
1976. 59 x 56 cm.

The conflict he sees between the contemporary and the mythical rages unabated in his soul and body. For him it is a mission of the greatest moment to unite the two. He is an artist out of supreme necessity.

The "Tree of Life" is a complex primeval symbol. With its roots deep in the loam of the subconscious and its crown stretching upwards to the sun and stars, the tree is the abode of paradoxical truths. Tribal cultures see the roots of the tree of the universe as the home of their fathers, whilst the crown serves as a repository for the tribal collective soul out from which spring new generations.

According to the Jewish book of wisdom, the Zohar, Man originally served God according to one creed and with all his heart. Death, sin and decay only took over when Man and his following departed from the Tree of Life. But one day the People and the Tree will once more be at one with each other and the Lord will banish Death and wipe away the tears from every face.

One day, all tribes, peoples and races will assemble in peace under the great Acacia Tree, as one African prophecy proclaims.

The trees of Life, of Knowledge and of Death – the Cross, or Tree of Crist, are all intermingled. Norse mythology's ambivalent view of the world is unfolded in the Yggdrasil. The tree in which Odin hung was the tree of Fate – of Metamorphosis; the tree of death and the subconscious, of wisdom and rejuvenation. The Tree of Life is to be found planted in the very soul of the peoples of India, Africa, Mexico, Scandinavia and the Middle East.

The idea of the Tree took shape in the mind of Ernst Neizvestny in the mid-nineteen fifties and grew out of the chaos and despair which marked this period in his life. One night in a particularly depressed state of mind, he caught his first glimpse of the "Tree of Life".

Today he sees it rising three hundred, even five hundred feet into the sky, as much an organic structure as a sculptural artifact. Preferably resting on the bottom of a slight depression in the landscape, it will wind away and up into space in the form of seven spiralling columns each in one of the seven colors of the spectrum. Together they become an open heart-shaped structure. This is filled not only with a multitude of figures, reliefs and paintings in a variety of materials, but also with kinetic

From one of the seven "Tree of Life" albums. This bears the title "Gigantomachia", which has associations with the hellenistic Pergamon frieze. Each album contains 28 pages, format: 15 x 40 cm. Two albums are in black and white, five in color.

12

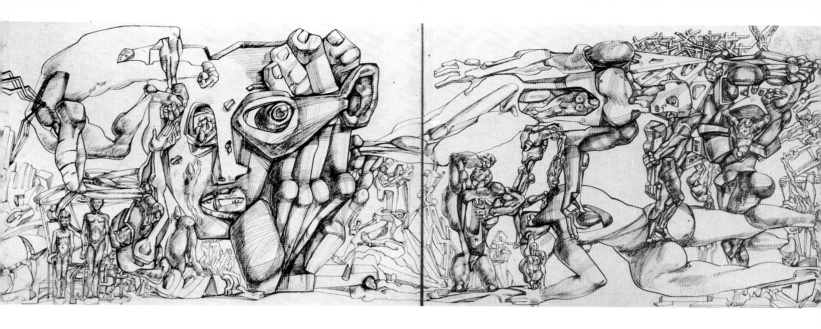

contrivances, mobiles, filmed displays, lighting effects and creative devices of all kinds. The central figure in this gigantic heart-like structure is Neizvestny's «Prophet» worked in bronze, emptying his breast with powerful hands.

Seven roots stretch down into the ground, one for each of the seven deadly sins. They form a system of tunnels – a labyrinth.

Spread over the ground like rays of light, seven roads of initiation lead into the monument. Travelling along any of them, the twentieth century's "Tree of Life" is first seen in the far distance, after which the visitor then comes to an opening shaped like one of the letters of the alphabet. Having passed through this – the Word, the Gateway to all Understanding, the inside of the monument comes into view revealing its multiplicity of open linear shapes with accompanying kaleidoscopic visual impressions. On a band circumscribing the Tree itself is engraved a biblical prayer of universally valid content written in four world languages.

Up the monument's central axis elevators will carry visitors to the seven levels of the structure. Every floor and ceiling will be transparent enabling all to see upwards, downwards and to every side.

Neizvestny refers to the theory that the Temple of Solomon was a model of the Universe. The temple was however a closed architectonic room with an exterior and an interior. "The Tree of Life" has neither an inside nor an outside, which coincides with Neizvestny's concept of the two worlds, the material and the spiritual, and with modern conceptions of time and space.

The seven spirals are in their form inspired by the geometrical abstractions of August Ferdinand Mobius (1790–1868). As an expression of a hypothetical view of the way the universe is ordered, this structural arrangement is, according to Neizvestny, a typically modern symbolic representation of the world about us and beyond. He sees it as a manifestation of the infinite, the unbroken, both mathematically and in its form. Metaphysically it can be seen as an expression of what he calls the universe beyond.

"This work if of great importance to me as an artist because it provides hitherto untried possibilities for emotional stimulation," says Neizvestny. "The phenomenon of space is abolished. One can experience being inside and outside simultaneously.

13

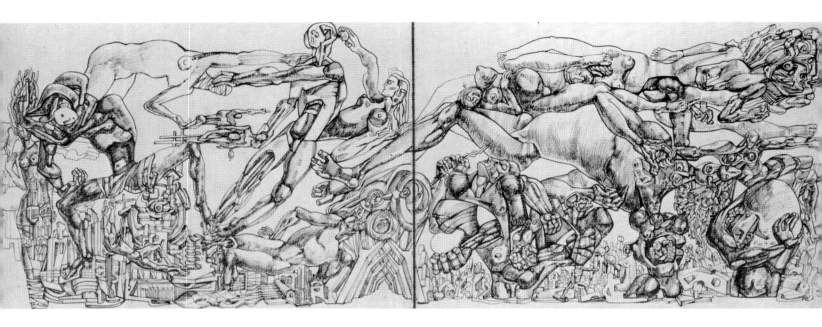

When a visitor is inside the sculpture he becomes a part of it and hence the stream of visitors is envisaged as a living part of the work. When they emerge, it is as if they are coming out of an eye or an ear. People move about inside a model of a living macrocosm and become integrated with it. It was indeed not without justification that the article in which John Russel, the art critic of the New York Times, introduced Neizvestny to his readers was given the title "Soviet sculptor thinks big".

At the beginning of the sixties, Ernst Neizvestny evolved the imagery which was to become an important part of the "Tree of Life". He filled albums with drawings and paintings, one for each of the spiral columns. The immediate impression one gets on examining these is that they are the fruits of an infinitely fertile visual imagination, and that their content, though enigmatic, is at the same time precisely determinable.

The imagery finds expression in a variety of artistic styles from fragmentary archaism and classicism, to semblances of surrealism, cubism, expressionism, minimalism, pop art and much more.

His thinking and his feelings are here succinct and concisely ethereal both in their formulation and in the way they affect his treatment of hollows and voids. This is to be seen in the painted glass, the reliefs, the slides and the film strips.

Into each other, round each other, after each other whirl male and female bodies, hands, masks, broken egg-shapes, science fiction fantasies and machine-like figures, totem poles and mythical animals. Realistic and abstract spectacles, dramatic and poetic scenes, dynamic movement and tranquility, steel and flesh, pregnancy and apocalypse, all spill out into space. One theme merges into another, but paradoxically, and in unexpected combinations without either end or beginning.

But the onlooker can interrupt this raging torrent and decide upon an overture, for example the head of a Venus torso out of which flows a stream of heroes and gods. And he can make up a coda in the form of a panorama of crucifixes, of a world that reminds one of Calvary. "Where is the beginning and where is the end of a spiral?" asks Neizvestny.

He envisages a continuation of the creative processes behind the "Tree of Life". In certain sections of it there is room enough for other artists to give shape to their own emotions and ideas both during his lifetime and after. He also intends to find space for

"Minotaur". Acrylics and oil. Motifs from the albums.

Exploding head. 1979–82. (1,11 x 1,73 m. This is a format which is standard for most of the paintings reproduced in this book.)

14

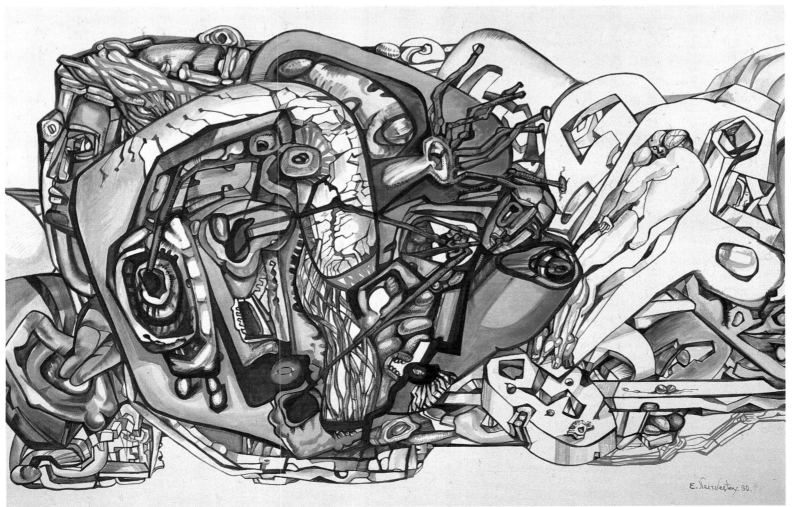

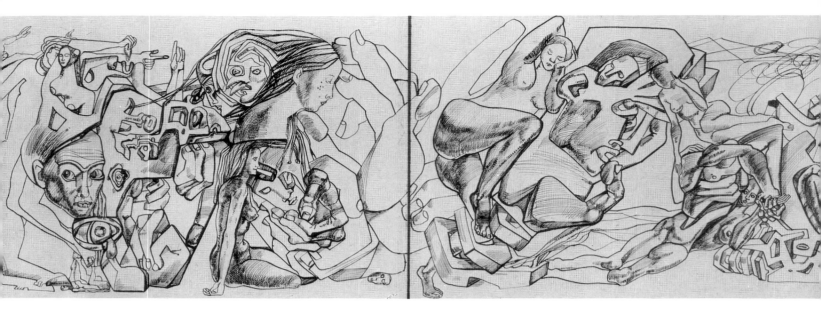

continually changing exhibitions and demonstrations of scientific and technical innovations.

A recurrent theme in the albums, with their mass of symbols and metaphors would appear to be the struggle between the forces of life and those of a demonic mechanised civilisation. The female is here the personification of human values whilst the male is more often than not a symbol of destructive, metallic precision. The naked figures of Adam and Eve in this scenario for the "Tree of Life" show Adam encased in a machine-like mask while Eve retains her smooth femininity. Adam's mask exudes machinery. The man develops into a semi-robot but the woman, still naked, remains unchanged.

One album in black and white opens with a drawing of one of two hands pointing upwards and filling with slowly falling human bodies. The other hand, open, palm upward, is stretched out white and calm, bearing what seems to be the Apple of Learning complete with eye. This apparently represents the universally basic roles of male and female exemplified by the hand of the creative artist as against the fertile hand of Nature.

Our gaze turns to and follows a stylised driveway lined with metallic trees, their crowns shaped like eggs or eye-balls; a dreamlike, precisely formulated piece of imagery. From a face, tears of stone roll from one of the eye sockets. The other eye is formed when a loose elongated shape is slid into the space where the eye should have been. The shape is pushed further and forms an ear on the other side of a hand desperately clutching the face the lips of which are a loose fragment about to fall off. This symbolises, perhaps, our inconstant senses.

A man floats downwards, his open, pregnant belly bearing a woman; the hermaphrodite is one of the constantly recurring symbolic figures in Neizvestny's art. A woman, naked and pregnant carries a church in her womb. Enigmatic and authoritatively drawn figures with shapes that are both geometric and organic crowd past.

In a color album he has obtained stained glass effects using black outlines and gouache coloring in radiant green, red, dark blue and yellow patches. Here too are terrified, desperate face masks and hands. And horse heads with eyes like roses and pieces of machinery. A huge wild horse head spits out a triumphant male figure, arms

"Exploding egg". From the series "Strange births", an album from the "Tree of Life".

War motif from one of the "Tree of Life" albums.

16

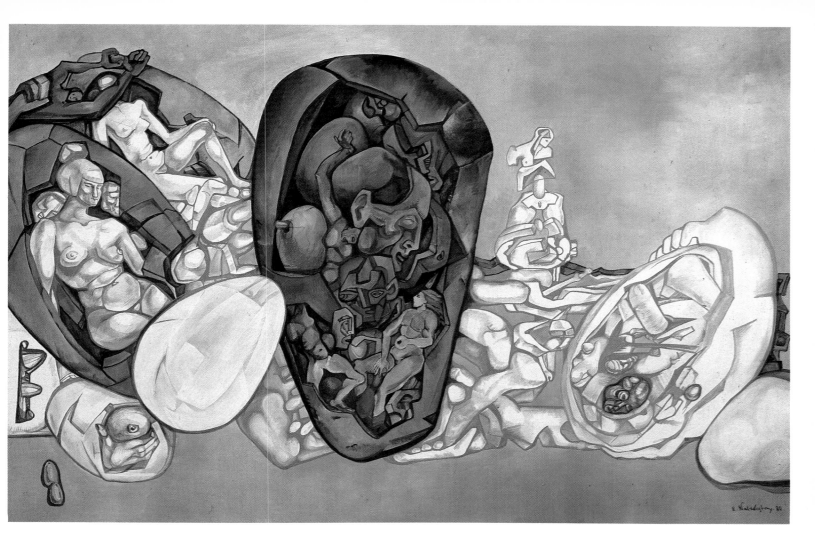

outstretched – the beginning of the apocalypse. The figure, thus ejected, lands in a mighty celestial hand where the man now a naked hero, appears in the middle of a circular blue aperture. This is followed by a spheroid in the center of which is the face of a child surrounded by fragments of geometric shapes. The dark sphere opens to emit an astronaut, a machine man with clenched metallic fists.

In the next frieze, blood red in color, a network of metallic shapes is projected outwards in a rhythmically exploding torrent. A terror-stricken child's face is glimpsed through the whirling masses. And out of this disarray stretches an open hand above which, over all the turmoil, hovers a butterfly.

The machine-like movement of the metallic tissues slows down to a calmer rhythm and the configurations become more clearly defined: heads with a cadaverous mien, putrefying faces, a kingdom of death. A man's visage, yellow in color, has lost its sight. Arteries gush blood from the eye sockets into an unattached eye. The blindness becomes yet another giant hand. From this emanates a thin powerful stream which can be the beginning of a new world, a new culture. A human figure has seemingly been born with a heart and hands among pieces of machinery harmoniously arranged. But once again there appears an astronaut, a crucifixion and blind faces of many different racial origins.

How are we to interpret this torrent of imagery and symbols from submerged layers of cultural consciousness and from ultra-modern contemporary sensibility? The wisdom that is stored in the innermost recesses of the mind of Mankind is an essence of myths and the metamorphosis of myths. When these vaults are breached the contents fly out and combine with the corresponding reality that surrounds Mankind. Out of this comes understanding. Is the eruption of visual imagery in the "Tree of Life" to be interpreted thus?

Ernst Neizvestny comments as follows:

"I do not see myself as a creator but as one who remembers. I have not yet awakened, but I am no longer asleep."

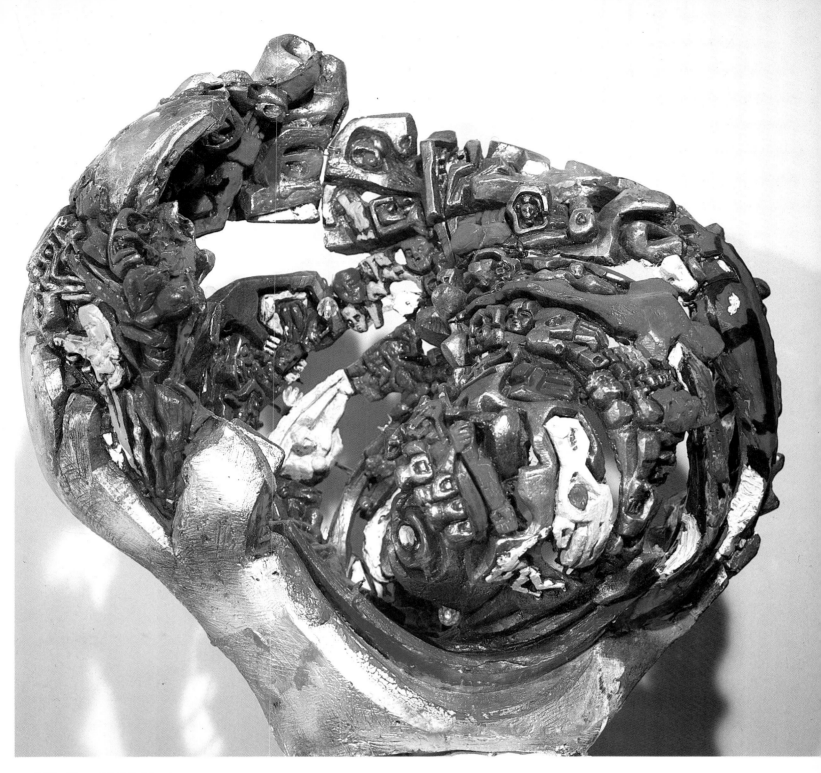

"The Tree of Life". Plastic
model in color. 54 x 56 cm.

In America

When Ernst Neizvestny moved into a studio on 79 Grand Street in 1977, he could hardly speak a word of English. But Soho, New York's international art village, was quick to embrace this thick-set eager character with dark piercing eyes which looked out at you over a pencil line of a moustache.

One of Neizvestny's first acquaintances was the owner of the neighbourhood grocery store, a Chinese with the very un-Chinese name of Bob. He and his wife ran the store in tiny box-like premises down the street.

The Russian newcomer made his purchases there every day, exchanging friendly greetings with Bob and his wife using nothing but signs and gestures.

One day the sculptor came into the store while the owner was out. The Chinaman's wife was busy serving a great hulk of a man who suddenly got mad about something or other and spat in her face. Without a moment's hesitation Neizvestny who had seen everything, repayed this disgustingly insulting behaviour with a right hook to the man's jaw. Thus it was that the lightweight drove the heavyweight out of the store. Neizvestny went home to his work. A while later he noticed that a street gang with the ill-mannered giant in their midst was hanging about in a menacing manner outside his studio which had no back door. There was little point in calling up the New York police on the telephone – in Russian, so Neizvestny rang some of his Russian friends and went back to work.

The doorbell rang. Neizvestny grabbed something he could use as a stick and opened the door. Outside stood a crowd of Chinese, Bob among them. Not an enemy in sight. Chinatown was only a few blocks away and when it comes to trouble the Chinese have a way of sticking together that others can have every reason to fear.

An oriental studio party was improvised on the spot. There were thanks and sweetmeats from the store, and the Russian was assured that he had only to let Chinatown know the next time he needed help.

He had another friendly contact with the Chinese quarter in New York five years later in the winter of 1982, and this time there was no question of needing help of any kind. The nearby Mao Gallery asked him to show some of his work there. He also received an invitation to visit Taiwan and exhibit his work there.

The episode in the Chinese store underscores one of the keynotes of Neizvestny's life, which is also reflected in his art. The British art historian John Berger studied him in Moscow in 1962. Later, he wrote in an article that Neizvestny's "main theme is courage", as it is expressed in the power of the will over the body.

But Ernst Neizvestny is, in the extreme sense of the phrase, a man of contrasts.

In April 1981 he invited me to come and stay with him for a few weeks. They were to be working weeks. The studio in tumble-down Grand Street was a former factory building, eighty feet long and twenty wide with a twenty foot ceiling. The walls were of white painted brick and the ceiling brownish planks covered with huge flame-

"The Prophet". Bronze. Modelled in 1962 in Moscow, and envisaged as the central figure in the "Tree of Life". Later, replaced by another conception of the prophet finished in the USA (see page 181 (1,30 x 1 m). The two pieces of sculpture give an idea of the way in which Neizvestny's style developed from his Moscow period to the seventies and eighties in New York.

colored acrylic paintings as well as numerous prints. The room itself was a petrified forest of sculptures in plaster, bronze, wood and zinc. There were statuettes and trial models of monuments both from his Soviet period and from five busy years in exile, scattered around all over the place. This was were Ernst Neizvestny lived and worked amidst a concentrate of his production, much in the way he one day hopes to live in his "Tree of Life".

In an attic room, with birds-eye view of his collected and still proliferating works, he had his ascetic bed, women visitors, an orthodox New Testament on the bedside table, a revolver in the drawer and a TV at the foot of the bed.

His guest had brought his winter clothes with him from the cold of Norway uncertain as he was of New York's fickle April weather. He had good use for all of them, mainly because the landlord was blatantly stingy with the central heating. The vast draughty studio was more like a refrigerator than anything else, not that its permanent occupant, brought up as he was in the Urals, noticed it. The freeze was part of the landlord's strategy of making life as miserable as possible for his tenant. The lease of the studio had gradually become less profitable. This was so because Soho's relatively new-found position as the Mecca of Modernism was driving rents higher every month. But despite the fact that Neizvestny had agreed to an increase in the rent, the threats of dispossession were kept up with a variety of expedients. At all times of the day or night the landlord would walk into the apartment to announce a new house rule or to convey some kind of criticism in an unpleasant tone of voice. The electric light would unexpectedly be switched off at the main. One day workmen marched in and set up a partition which reached up to the ceiling and blocked out the daylight. A rock group was persuaded to occupy the cellar and to play at full blast all through the night.

The position in which Neizvestny found himself was by no means unique in the Soho of the day. After the war, artists had begun to move into the empty stock rooms, attics and closed-down factories, complete with old-fashioned goods elevators, of this back-end of Lower Manhattan, named not after London's Soho, but because it lay "south of Houston Street", beyond Greenwich Village.

In the course of 25–30 years this whole area developed into one of the world's biggest centers of avant-garde art. Some of the mondane galleries in 57th Street and Madison Avenue, even found it worthwhile to open a branch down here among the myriad galleries for primitive, exotic and experimental art. The whole district is picturesquely genuine, and boasts New York's largest collection of 19th century cast iron house fronts, a building practice peculiar to the United States. Here the artists paid modest rents while the whole quarter dozed happily. Some of the artists won international recognition and turned the place into a world attraction with unfortunate consequences for their colleagues in the form of increased real estate values and

The artist in his studio at 78 Grand Street in Soho, New York

22

prices. Restaurants, boutiques, fashion houses and other businesses now proceeded to outbid the artists and threatened to squeeze them out of the district. This was the reason why a local association had been formed to protect the interests of the artists who lived there.

Was this association not somewhere Neizvestny could have turned to for help? By no means. Neizvestny was perfectly prepared to take the consequences of capitalist liberalism even when it worked in his disfavor. He is intensely sceptical and adamant about collectives and especially of artists associations. "They begin so well, and their intentions are of the best. But they always end up as bureaucratic organisations where certain types of person start ruling the roost, stifling the freedom of those who need to enjoy it."

He preferred to conduct the trivial battle with his lilleputian landlord through a lawyer, or preferably through direct negotiation.

As a rule he met insults and pinpricks with good-humored politeness. Of no small relevance to the psychological side of the whole affair is that the villain of the piece, apart from playing the role of a minor capitalist, was also a dabbler in the arts in the nonfigurative minimal style. However, apart from the odd explosive utterance, Neizvestny remained unaffected by his aggressive behaviour.

"It reminds me of the Soviet mentality, of the art world's loyal party careerists and of the KGB," he observed. "The KGB would have been overjoyed had I ranted at them, fought back and allowed myself to be provoked. But I made monuments for them instead of playing politics the way a Solzhenitsyn did," conveniently forgetting to mention his famous row with Khrushchev in 1962 as he made this assertion. "All I wanted was to work as a free artist. Why get so mad?" he smiled, bursting with the answer to his rhetorical question.

He regarded his landlord as a reminder of the ever-present petit bourgeois mentality in our world. "The problems he makes for me are small. He helps me remember how small they are."

This aloofness from the trivial and the ephemeral is very marked both in his way of life and in his artistic temperament. In his case it springs from a metaphysical consciousness which has its roots in a conversance with death which stretches right back to his earliest childhood and which was later to be reinforced as a result of what happened to him in the Soviet Union in both the real war and the cold one that followed.

The contrast is an enigma, as is the connection between his basic view of life as being transient and full of illusion, and the way he identifies with bodily pain, sensuality, violence and vulgarity. His form world bulges with passionate bullish strength. This is the dominant quality of his sculpture, though his perspective stretches far beyond such vitalism.

24

Female torso. Acrylic and oil. 1977–80.

His need for freedom makes him willing to accept the West's accelerating pluralism as it is reflected in contemporary art.

But in the midst of all the tensions in his life, he seeks with all his might to achieve a totality, a synthesis – a "Tree of Life".

"I have no wish to compare myself with the great. Picasso has taken the whole machinery to pieces. My task is to reassemble the bits, but on another plane. I am of the opinion that analysis in art has been taken far enough. Now is the time to synthesise," he said to me in an interview I had with him in Switzerland shortly after he had left the Soviet Union.

The consequences for his form language of this view has caused several critics and art dealers to regard him as a borrower who has lifted from a Henry Moore, a Zadkine, Lipchitz, Picasso, of course, and more.

But Ernst Neizvestny is after something different; after something more. His composite style enables him to give visual expression to a multifaceted subject through the highly imaginative use of a variety of styles, metaphors, associated ideas and symbols from the mythological past down to our time. Without an eclectic style such as his, an epic work such as the "Tree of Life" would be unthinkable.

He knows full well that content must be at one with form.

Crucifix. Acrylic and oil. 1977–80. One of Neizvestny's numerous variations of the crucifix motif. They cannot always, indeed should not always, be seen in a religious light, since they often symbolise other forms of conflict in life and society.

"I am convinced that it is possible in art to find laws that apply not only to art itself, but also to human activity and to Nature."

Among his favourite motifs are the crucifix in countless variants, hermaphrodites, dinosaurs, masks and, most of all, centaurs. Remote from our world, this latter creature, part horse, part man, trots through Greek mythology in the orgiastic company of Dionysius, the god of fertility and conqueror of death. In art a subject no longer of interest. Except to Neizvestny. And Picasso, by the way.

"Sculpture is more than just plastic elements. The interesting thing about sculpture is what happens in between the elements, in the union of contrasts.

It is not difficult when you do the same as the academically oriented and start with the human body. A body is a body. But when it comes to a centaur, things start to happen that interest me – a union of two different bodies, and out of this comes energy such as is generated when things are complicated. The establishment of unity between polarities, between the static and the dynamic, the organic and the geometric, the abstract and the realistic, between idea and form, is what concerns me as a sculptor."

It is perhaps not so strange that some would like to regard Neizvestny as a spiritualist, a renewer of Christian art, whilst yet others are taken with the vitalism in his work.

He himself is a centaur, with the Bible on his bedside table and Eros in his bed. Crucifix and sexual symbol. They are the two extremes of Neizvestny's gamut of passion. Khrushchev, man of the people, saw him thus. "There is both an angel and a devil in you."

The two extremes drive him forward. The balance between them is never the same. The totality of his identity, his universe, is always under threat and must be recreated

26

again and again. He finds this same pattern of conflict throughout the history of art in different civilisations. He sees it more than anywhere else in the threat from mechanisation and standardisation to the spiritual and the humane in our contemporary society.

He sits on the low couch in the studio and arches his back as he makes a spontaneous confession. "I often have the feeling that there is an angel, or a demon, sitting on my back and riding me like a horse. It is as if it is not I who am being driven from one task in my studio to another. For a while my assistant thought me a little cracked; that I was rushing restlessly about to no purpose. I told him that I had the great "Tree of Life" project on my mind all the time and that all my work, paintings as well as sculpture were tied up with it. It was no different, I said, to when he was working on one painting and added detail after detail to it. Then he understood.

What I didn't tell him about was the angel on my shoulder guiding me. This is something I really have experienced and it is sometimes rather uncanny."

Is it possible for a Russian of Neizvestny's make-up to become acclimatized to the stresses and strains of New York? He is really happy in his new surroundings. He is in his element, despite having to build up a new career after the age of fifty.

What has he lost?

"Everything," is his answer, as he thinks back to his intimate environment in Moscow, his large circle of friends and the eight hundred bronzes and scale models in other materials which he had to leave behind him in the Soviet Union.

The position of leadership at home that he so dramatically occupied in his capacity as a world famous sculptor was no starting point for a career on the other side of the Atlantic.

But he gets excited about the freedom and the continually changing conditions that are to be found in American life. He has seen many Russian exiles with a deep-rooted cultural consciousness who are unhappy in the United States. They cannot satisfy their need for cultural stimulation amongst all the widespread and irrepressible vulgarity.

Maybe it is also a question of feelings that are different from esthetics and a longing for a cultural environment. Arthur Miller, the writer, who incidentally is an acquaintance of Ernst Neizvestny from the time they met in Moscow, tells in his book of Russian impressions, published in 1969, of a woman interpreter who had been in the United States several times and admired a great deal there. But she asked: "When everyone in America thinks first and foremost of their own advantage, how can you keep things rolling?" A good question, thought Miller, and answered with another question. "When all this (meaning the Soviet Union) is governed by a handful of men, how can you keep it rolling?" He sensed that "she felt there to be a strong centrifugal force within both herself and her fellow countrymen which would hurl everything out into space unless it were kept under strict control."

This intuitive feeling is confirmed in Nadezhda Mandelstam's memoirs. She was the widow of the poet Ossip Mandelstam, one of the victims of the Stalin régime. Looking back, she sees the Russian intelligentsia as being the accomplices of the Bolsheviks in their oppression of the people.

"There had been a time when all of us out of panic-stricken fear of chaos, prayed for a strong system of government, for a mighty hand which could hold back the raging tide of humanity which had burst all barriers. This fear of chaos was perhaps the most lasting of our feelings – we have not recovered from it yet and it is carried through from generation to generation. In our blindness we ourselves have fought to establish regimentation, because in every difference of opinion, in every disagreement, we saw the beginnings of fresh anarchy and chaos. And either by our silence or by our acceptance we have helped the system to gain strength and defend itself against those who oppose it."

Whatever opinion we may have of Neizvestny's struggle for a place in the sun as a creative artist in the Soviet Union, and there are several, he has not for one moment shared the fear of freedom. That is why he is so well disposed towards the dynamism and will to suceed that it is to be found in the United States. But of course he is not unaware of the drawbacks of a society in which such attitudes prevail.

We are sitting in a new Italian restaurant in Soho – new cafés and art galleries are springing up every week, much to Neizvestny's delight.

He draws the constellation of law and order as a straight line on his serviette. Up against it he traces a circle of anarchy, the free play of forces. Sometimes the one dominates the scene, sometimes the other. This state of tension is always dangerous, and it is always there. It is America and it is life: the state of tension between freedom and order.

"When I came to Western Europe I was the guest of the richest men, of presidents and cardinals. I held exhibitions and sold well. But all the time I had the feeling that I wasn't living my own life, that I was watching a film. When I came to New York it was quite different. A man who lives in Soho is a real human being. His clothes suit the conditions under which he lives. The first months I was over here I lived on Park Avenue with some wealthy relatives. Park Avenue is for the rich, the really rich. Harlem is where the poor, the really poor, live. I don't mean to say that this state of affairs is a boon to society, but contrasts such as these, this sort of rhythm is very close to the rhythm of my own nature. I feel like an American who has been abroad for a very long time, has forgotten the language, and is now back again."

Neizvestny has discovered that he can no longer remember the names of those he went to school with. And unlike most war veterans, he cannot recall specific war-time experiences or encounters and not even particular officers or men.

I haven't got an eye here," he says, pointing to the back of his head. He never looks back, does not suffer from nostalgia for the Soviet Union. I remark on the fact that I have hardly found one landscape, one tree, one flower, one mountain in all his innumerable drawings, prints and paintings. Neizvestny admits to having no roots in Russian nature, in fact not in any kind of landscape. He takes pleasure in experiencing deserts, Scandinavian winters, Swiss alps. But he feels at home in none of them. "My life is like a stream, it flows from the present and into the future, unhampered by time or place."

And yet another confession: "Existence is like a dream. I have always had the feeling that somewhere near at hand is a rich life, and that one day I shall wake up and live it."

His mother is Jewish. He left Russia on a Jewish passport. He has supported Israel's cause in the United States by producing numerous copies of a bronze statuette symbolising the twelve lost tribes. He has also decorated ceramic works with Jewish symbols for sale in aid of Israel. But how does he feel about a Jewish identity?

"Jews come to my studio in Grand Street and ask: Why all these crucifixes?

Russians who come, ask: How can you be so very fond of America? Don't you love Russia? Aren't you a patriot?

Christians ask: Why are you not a member of the Orthodox Church, or that and that church? And they think: How much does Jewry mean to him?

"To take the Jewish question first", continues Neizvestny. "I support the Jewish cause, and I try to help Jews in need. As one of the three main branches of the "Tree of Life", I have in mind the twelve tribes of Israel. They symbolise the progress of the generations of mankind through history. But I am thinking in the biblical sense, where Israel and Christ are universal. And of course I feel that I am naturally free to criticise Jews and their actions when I find reason to do so, just as I do where other individuals, peoples or nations are concerned.

And I love Russia. I have nearly bled to death for Russia. But I have never been able to accept the communist system.

America, with its freedom, with all its immense and deeply tragic contrasts, satisfies something central to my artistic temperament, to my basic view of life."

At a number of universities from Columbia and Yale to Berkley and Stanford, Neizvestny has given lectures with the help of slides and an interpreter, on the "Tree of Life" and his synthesis-oriented views, accompanied by comments on American phenomena.

Russian intellectuals sometimes find Americans naive and primitive. They claim that they betray themselves by their questions. According to Neizvestny this is an unfair conclusion. The difference lies in what they have experienced.

"Americans experience things in a more normal way than I experience them. For example, a hunchback will know more about women than a normally built man

*Metallic hermaphrodite.
Acrylics and oil. 1980. The
hermaphrodite theme recurs
often. According to
Neizvestny, hermaphrodites are
ambivalent figures in which
there exists a state of tension
between opposites such as male
and female, man and machine
etc.*

because he as a rule will find it more difficult to attract them. But it is the well-formed person who is normal, not the hunchback.

Americans ask naive question because they are normal. How can for example an American student be expected to understand that a person in Russia who is discovered to be a homosexual, risks getting ten years in prison. Or that we must always carry identity papers in our own country. He just does not comprehend."

But Neizvestny deplores the current trend in American universities towards pragmatism and over-specialisation. "For example, it is amazing to come upon a specialist on Dostoyevsky who does not research all Dostoyevsky. Instead he is a specialist on Dostoyevsky's left nostril. He knows everything about it. But when he comes up against a problem which has to do with Dostoyevskys right nostril, he has to turn for help to a specialist on that subject."

The professors in the art departments in the various universities are often mediocre artists, according to Neizvestny's observations. He senses that for this reason they plan their courses in such a way as to be able to justify their work. "They make art out to be so complex that it is practically incomprehensible. But the task of the teacher is to simplify the complex and to make it intelligible. American professors of art often do the opposite. They lecture on an endless number of pseudo-theories about the simplest of problems."

But Neizvestny has a soft spot for students. "You can criticise them, you can bawl them out, you can put forward provocative views that are in open conflict with theirs. They are open, make a sport out of debate and appreciate a strong opponent.

But I must add that art students, at least those with whom I had the closest contact, often seem to find themselves at a dead end. Maybe that was the reason why my theories about synthesis in the arts were so often received with enthusiasm."

"Could the feeling have anything to do with what so many have been contending, namely that American contemporary art has landed up a blind alley?"

"It is difficult to say. The various modernist movements were inspired by brilliant masters. However, these could maybe be compared to the kind of ram that leads his sheep to the slaughterhouse. These rams do alright, they win honour and make money. But the sheep go under because they sought security with the rams."

"But such a view says nothing of the nature of these various movements, nor of the extent to which the American art scene has produced really creative artists. How do you see these aspects from your point of view?"

"This is something I cannot be sure of. I don't know all the aspects of the American art scene. But I have noticed something rather important in a field that has held particular interest for me. American art historians and critics are familiar with the formal and constructivist side of Russian avantgardism. But they are not conscious of the foundations upon which it was built during the years before and after the October Revolution. For this reason they cannot entirely understand what I, the avantgardists' successor, am trying to do.

Russian avantgardism was based on widely understood methaphysics. From Vladimir Tatlin, the prophet of constructivism, to Yusikochsky, the father of Russian rocketry, the technical achievements of many Russians were founded on metaphysical concepts. It is characteristic that a philosopher such as Nikolai Feyodorov was an inspiration to some of them. He was a Christian believer whose conception of the world was one of universal atonement. He considered technical progress to be deeply meaningful. The advent of the new technological civilisation meant the realisation of God's purpose which was that mankind, as his instrument, should dominate the earth. Technology was part of God's plan for creation.

These and other related spiritualistic impulses inspired a Tatlin, a Malevich and

most of all Wassily Kandinsky. In this context I see myself as a pupil, not an epigone, of the Russian avantgardists."

To support this argument Ernst Neizvestny uses the cross symbol in the same way as he does on so many other occasions.

"Art is in the sign of the cross, by which I mean that if we can envisage that the eternal mysteries of life form the vertical axis of the cross, whilst the current problems of our contemporary society form the horizontal axis, then at the point of intersection lies the truth, great art and literature: Dante, Dostoyevsky, Rabelais, the temples, Michelangelo . . .."

"But we were talking about American art."

"Take that most American of all impulses, Pop Art. I have been fascinated by it. Its courage conquered snobbism and assimilated much of what was popular and vulgar in the lives of the majority of the people. But the pop artists went no further. They were prisoners of the horizontal and lost sight of the vertical. The pop artists were the children of the big city, not of the universe. This is the reason why Pop Art is a blind alley. They regarded art merely as a phenomenon after Duchamp, after Dada. They have, for example no feeling for Stone-age art. To them it does not exist. Their art is outside history, free from esoteric problems. But it is good art.

I am accused of being without principle. People do not understand how I can accept so much. But at a time when there is no common style the modern artist must be prepared to start from scratch and acquaint himself with the means that civilisation has at its disposal. When I see an abstract work, I like it. When I see Pop Art and Op Art, I like them too. That's because I see them as contributing to a whole. I see how everything belongs in a universal work, in the 'Tree of Life'."

Once again, this idea of the "Tree of Life". How and when was its seed planted in Ernst Neizvestny? This is a story that is as long as his life.

Childhood

What sort of a place was the industrial town of Sverdlovsk east of the Urals, when Ernst Neizvestny was a child? The naked face of Stalinism was showing itself as the first steps were taken in 1932 towards the complete regimentation of art and literature and, a year later, as the terror collectivisation of the peasantry was begun.

In the Spring of 1934, Ossip and Nadezhda Mandelstam were on their way to Soviet Asia under a special deportation order from Stalin.

They had been sitting all day long in the waiting hall of the Sverdlosk railroad station in the hope of getting a connection. All this time they had been given nothing to eat or drink. They were placed on a bench right in front of the main entrance between two grim-faced armed guards. An endless stream of people passed by close to where they sat. All looked the other way. None looked back.

They continued their journey through the Urals in crowded trains and ferries. Not a soul, either child or adult, would look the two political prisoners in the eye. All this apparent indifference saddened the arrested writer. "In Tsarist times, they gave alms to prisoners. Now they don't even look at them."

There was, however, another far less obvious side to Sverdlovsk and it was within the confines of this that Ernst Neizvestny grew up and enjoyed a good and richly stimulating childhood right in the middle of a reign of terror.

Before the Revolution Sverdlovsk was called Yekaterinburg after Empress Catherine the Second. It had been built as a fortified frontier town in the 17th century and was later to win a unique position as a bastion of freedom. Up through the Tsarist period, it became a sort of permanent stopping off place for political and criminal deportees who had served their sentences but whom the authorities were anxious not to have back in central Russia.

This practice continued after the October Revolution. Sverdlovsk remained a haven for one-time aristocrats and bourgeois revolutionaries, for communist devia-

Ernst and his cousin Jakov in Cossac uniform.

Family portrait. Ernst second from the left between his mother and grandmother. His father is standing behind him.

tionists and freed criminals. Many of these brought with them the fellowship and mutual trust that had been developed during the years of imprisonment and exile. People of various professions and trades, beliefs and social backgrounds crossed swords with each other in the privacy of their homes, and all the while the totalitarian régime spread its tentacles about them with ever growing brutality and efficiency. These people became involved in endless discussions among themselves in an atmosphere of complete freedom such as Ernst Neizvestny was not to experience later on in his life.

This closely knit Sverdlovsk community where opinions could be aired on the highest level and with absolute discretion, was Neizvestny's model for the "catacomb culture" which he organised after the war among Moscow's diffuse and carefully watched intelligentsia. There was at that time a lack of contact between various academic disciplines that ought to have been able to cross-fertilise one another, and he sees a similar state of affairs as beeing a weakness in American cultural life today.

He remembers Sverdlovsk as an exciting town, not least because it was a meeting place for the cultures of Europe and Asia, for Russians and Tartars and Chinese, of which there were many still to be seen when he was a child. A place, in short, after his own heart.

In the Yekaterinburg of old, not all those who had been freed, were interested in disclosing their previous identities. It was said that now and again someone would introduce himself as "the unknown" or "the anonymous one" – in Russian "neizvest-ny". This is at any rate the explanation which Ernst Neizvestny gives offhand as the origin of his peculiar name. Another version which has been suggested in Jewish quarters among others, is that the name has its origin in the 19th century when tsarist agents were said to have kidnapped Jewish youths, forced them to become Christians and consigned them to a long period of military training and service. Their names were taken away from them, their officers giving them fresh and often original ones. It is claimed that one such was Neizvestny.

Those sections of the intelligentsia which had not found favor with the new régime, not to mention ordinary working class people, were, according to numerous accounts, housed in the years after the revolution under the most crowded conditions conceivable in such cities as Moscow and Leningrad. Not so, in far away Sverdlovsk. Ernst Neizvestny and his nine years younger sister grew up in a spacious three-storey house with a garden. He had his own nursery and a nursemaid. In the middle of the house was an irreplaceable treasure chest of a library with a good solid collection of pre-Revolution books, scientific as well as fiction and non-fiction.

On his father's side, Ernst Neizvestny gives as his antecedents a great grandfather who served for a quarter of a century as an officer in the army of the Tsar and a grandfather who was a wealthy capitalist and the owner of a large printing works. His father Ossip (Joseph) Neizvestny, together with two brothers took part in the Civil War on the White Russian side. This background made things difficult for his son Ernst as he grew up. And it prevented Ossip from completing his medical training in either Moscow or Leningrad. He had to take his final examination at a provincial medical school in Tomsk.

He was a meticulous person. He dressed correctly with high collar, well-polished shoes and spats. Like a "Salvador Dali" is how his son remembers him. His whole mentality was completely and utterly anti-proletarian. He was courageous and outspoken. The local secret police warned him on several occasions, but spared him, presumably because of his medical skill and his political harmlessness, the result of his hopelessly upper-class background.

He was not well-to-do, neither was he poor. Ernst Neizvestny can only remember one occasion when his parents discussed money matters in the home. Otherwise conversation and discussions were concerned with a wide range of cultural, political, artistic and psychological subjects.

His father was conservative in his general outlook, but tolerant, with interests extending from history and politics to technical matters and sport. He was athletic, a champion dancer, a good figure skater, billiards champion of the Urals and Siberia and something of a gambler. He was his son's athletics trainer.

The boy liked his father, but thought him very old-fashioned, a character out of Dickens.

"But the older I get, the more I see my father in myself, right down to the physical characteristics."

His mother on the other hand was a liberal and a democrat, a Western European bohemian. She was much taken up with religion and theosophy, with Madame Blavatsky and Annie Besant, with Rudolf Steiner's anthroposophy and with Tibetan mysticism.

She is Russian born, of Jewish-French parentage. Her maiden name is Bella Dejour.

On the ninth of April 1926, she gave birth to a son to whom she gave the name Erik Josifovitch, the Erik from a saga about a Nordic king. But since the name in Russian has, according to Neizvestny, childish associations, he changed it to Ernst when he grew up.

The child was late in starting to talk, so late that his parents began to get worried. But his tongue loosened at last and he began to talk and read at about the same time. His nursemaid, who was to come into his life at a later date in a miraculous fashion, read aloud to him from illustrated children's books. The child followed the printed words and understood them through the pictures. He used this same method when he came to the United States and had to learn English. He studied the funnies and assimilated words and pictures at the same time.

36

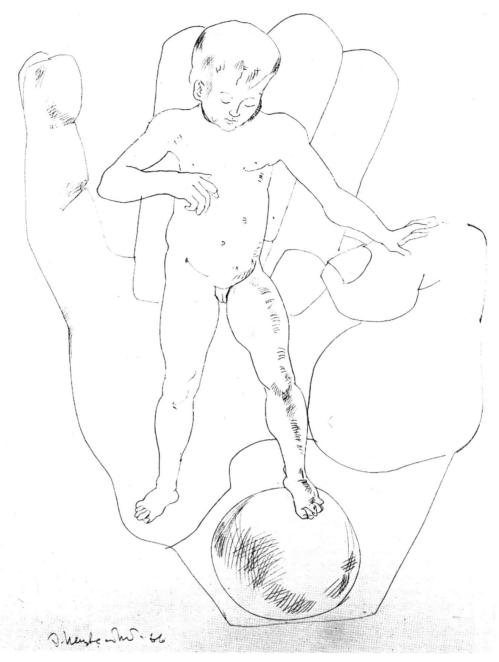

The early age at which he overcame his illiteracy and the speed with which it happened, resulted in his being able to read *Don Quixote* fluently by the time he started school and other children were learning the ABC. For this reason he was sent home for a while. When he was recalled, the class had also learnt to write and do arithmetic, this latter being something that he never came to learn to do properly.

His mother had studied bio-chemistry at the University of Leningrad in her younger days. She was a follower of a genetic school which was banned under Stalin. She lost her status as a scientist but, in the privacy of her own home, continued with her experiments using such animals as guinea pigs, rabbits and birds camouflaged as little Erik's zoo. The child was an eager helper with these experiments – his first meeting with underground science.

His mother went on to become a writer and wrote childrens books which came to be widely known in the Soviet Union and were translated into German, Japanese and Polish. She also wrote lyric poetry and was caught up in ecological and environmental protection movements. In the sixties she published a book in which she had the animals complain about the ruthless way men exploited them and despoiled Nature.

"I understand today far more clearly than I did when I was young, how much my parents have meant to me. I don't think they had any definite ideas as to how I should be brought up," recollects Neizvestny. "But the whole environment in my childhood home – the library, the general tone in the family circle, the people who came to visit us for varying lengths of time, all helped to mould me.

Every Saturday my father would have a number of people in to play cards, debate, eat good food and drink vodka. They were all professional men of various kinds and of different political persuasions. They had known each other for a long time. Among them were engineers and scientists. One of them was a very gifted mathematician, another, the manager of a company, an officer in the Red Army and a convinced communist. They kept it going all night into Sunday, sometimes even into the following night with only one or two hours sleep before they had to start work on the Monday morning. I was allowed to stay up too, although I cannot have been more than ten or eleven years old. This was something I knew my mother did not approve of.

Arguments would start on any of a whole variety of subjects, often with far-reaching historical, scientific and economic perspectives. Only religion would my father not discuss. He considered religious discussions too complicated. If anybody broached this kind of subject he maintained an eloquent silence."

New ideas and thoughts whirled past the young boy's ears. He would run to his mother and ask how he could find out more about what he had heard. She found books for him in the family library. "That was my academy of life."

The conversational tone at the card table was blunt and outspoken. Once the communist made a mistake in dealing. "That creep Stalin must have taught you how to deal," was Neizvestny's father's comment.

"You don't understand Stalin," replied the communist, and started a huge argument on the subject of politics (and this at a time when just to hint at anything unfavorable about the Secretary of the Party even in the most private company, could easily lead to years of hard labour or a death sentence).

His father once remarked to another player: "Why are you scratching yourself all the time?" The question of psoriasis came up and he gave such a fascinating lecture on this skin disease that the listening boy became quite hypochondrical. He marched off and read all about psoriasis in the medical encyclopedia and was convinced that he was a sufferer. In all secrecy he visited one of his father's colleagues who found nothing wrong. His father had a good laugh when he heard about it.

"Boy". Bronze. 1954.
(0,90 x 0,52 m).

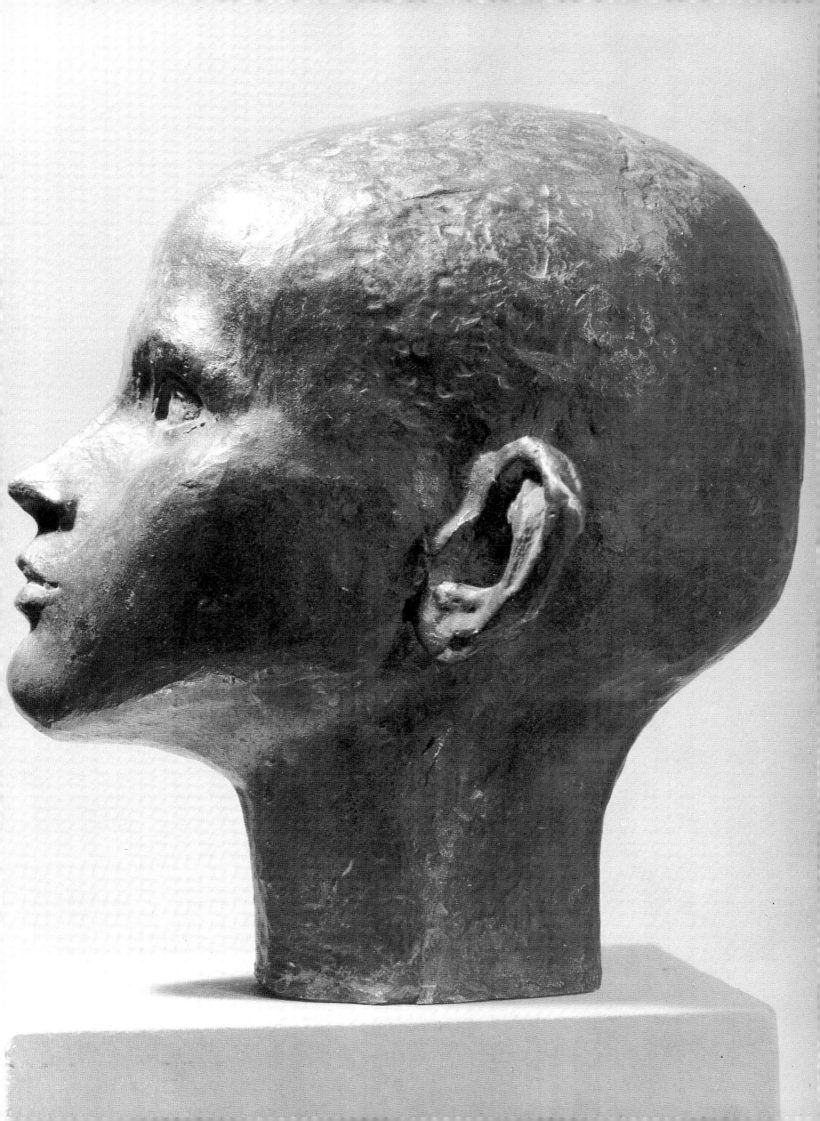

When his mother started to write, she came into contact with both official and dissident authors. One of these was an old friend, the lyric poet Nikolai Zapolotsky, a contemporary of Mandelstam and Akhmatova. There are some Russian critics to-day who rank him higher than Pasternak as a writer. This is at any rate Neizvestny's opinion. Bella Dejour had met him in her student days, and introduced Zapolotsky, newly returned from military service, into literary circles in the Leningrad of the early nineteen-twenties. They were even at one time engaged to be married.

Zapolotsky was sent to prison and was away for many years. But he managed to smuggle poems written in tiny handwriting out to Neizvestny's mother – dangerous documents in those days. She used her son as a memory bank for she made him learn the smuggled poems off by heart in order to preserve them.

By the time Zapolotsky was rehabilitated and once again a free man, Ernst Neizvestny was in his thirties. They met and Neizvestny, without faltering, recited the poems to the man who had written them and some of which he had quite forgotten. They appeared in print after Zapolotsky had reworked them.

His mother's interests also took in the unseen blushing flowers among the common people, some of whom came to make their mark on his childhood home.

For a time the authorities pressed his mother to travel about in the Urals and Siberia and give lectures – much against her own convictions – on the way modern science had discredited the accounts of the miracles in religious literature. Her husband teased her for doing this, but she somehow managed to reconcile this theme with her own theosophical and anthroposophical views.

On these trips she sought out local geniuses who she brought back with her to Sverdlovsk taking them into her home under her husband's ironic, but tolerant eye. Neizvestny remembers a great bear-like peasant lad whose speciality was singing in a woman's voice. He put on his mother's dresses, ate like a pig and tried to seduce her son.

A "peoples poet" came next. He is a fraud, said Neizvestny senior, locked everything moveable up in cupboards and drawers and was right. The people's poet stole everything he could lay his hands on and decamped.

A tiny man with a head like Peter the Great was given lodgings. He had been a political prisoner, was a follower of Leo Tolstoy's Christian ideas, and like the lady of the house was a vegetarian. His name was Giffelbein and he was engaged in writing a long treatise on Nature's mathematical laws. Ernst Neizvestny remembers him as something of a genius. This man later obtained an important post as an agro-biologist and regional product improver for the Urals and Siberia. But when Neizvestny's mother took him in, it was an act of courage on her part. He was a political outcast and it was even forbidden to mention his name. The first article to be published about him was written by Mrs. Neizvestny.

The post-impressionistic painter Felix Lembergsky came to the house in 1942 at Mrs. Neizvestny's invitation. He had avoided military service, was ill and had no food ration card. This at a time when the whole country was living close to starvation. But Lembergsky stayed with the Neizvestnys during the whole war time period, and longer, whilst his hosts exchanged furniture and valuables for potatoes to keep them all from starving.

41

In the meantime Ernst Neizvestny had become a teenager, keen on football and boxing, and a leader among his contemporaries. Whilst the painter Lembergsky passed away the hours lying on a sofa, his colleague-to-be longed to be called up for active military service, not, as he said, to defend communism, but to "make history" as his father once had done. His father laughed at him, and Ernst who volunteered for service only to be rejected, suspected his father of having had a word or two with the recruiting officer.

Doctor Neizvestny wanted his son to take up some sensible profession. In the Ural region the most respected men of science were the geologists, so he got him accepted for a four year course in geology at a local college which took students straight from school.

One of his mother's friends was a geologist and a member of the Academy of Science and he gave Ernst a brief grounding in the essentials of that science. As a result the lad found the elementary detail of the first year course deadly dull. He skipped school and went to the town's pioneer centre for young people where he was allowed to draw and paint.

"I soon became something of a curiosity there. All the others made pictures of landscapes and people while I preferred to draw skeletons, death and hands."

"Why skeletons?"

"I don't know. To put it simply, I was never particularly interested in the world around me, how a tree looked, but rather how a tree was. I was interested in what went on inside, in how things lived, more than in what Nature looked like.

I had a secret. As a child I liked to look at the window, not out of it mind you, when it was raining or snowing. I stared at it without blinking. Pictures would appear. Usually they were of myself as a grown-up. It was rather like the cinema, but they were fantasy pictures conjured up on the spot. There could be pictures in which I identified myself with Roald Amundsen, the explorer, or Paracelsius, or Spartacus surrounded by heroic warriors. I could see myself as Alexander the Great, or as Pasteur in different situations. One such was where I convinced Stalin in the Kremlin that the art he stood for was third-rate. The great martyrs among statesmen, among men of religion and science, as well as men of action, were all people of my world.

Gradually I learned how to do without the window when I called up these pictures, and could do so whenever I concentrated sufficiently. I can still, whenever I get bored, find myself a corner and start "seeing".

Neizvestny has described these lonely, but all-important hours of his childhood in a forthcoming book. In it, the boy Erik stands in wonder at the window and out in the snow of the future the worldly-wise Ernst answers his questioning gaze. "The boy often seems to me to be thinking more clearly than the grown man." But life as we know it is more than just poetry and fantasy. Every afternoon young Ernst would come home from the Palace of Culture and pretend that he had been attending his geology classes.

"Monsters and the defenseless Life". Etching from the series "Monarchia". 1967–74. This series of graphic works consists of about 100 prints. 65 x 31 cm.

"What have you learnt today?" questioned the voice of parental authority. The lad answered evasively. His mother saw through him and what could have developed into an extremely unpleasant situation, was suddenly resolved when young Ernst in competition with youngsters from all over the country won a place at a new Soviet elite school for artistically gifted children.

The school had been started by one of Stalin's men, Lazar Kaganovich, on principles that had been propounded in the time of Tsar Nicholas the First. Classes were at high school level with special emphasis on artistic subjects. The State paid all expenses. Each class consisted of no more than a handful of pupils who had fifteen teachers at their disposal.

The competition for places had been very keen and they had not been reserved for children from the privileged classes. That was how Ernst Neizvestny got in, despite his White Russian background. It was however, not long before parents who were among the privileged in the State, managed to get their children places at the school, and the witticism that it was a school for gifted parents became a standing joke.

For Neizvestny, now fourteen, this opportunity was to have a decisive influence on his life. He had modelled, drawn and painted for as long as he could remember. But he had also written poetry as well as having many other interests. He had had no special thoughts of becoming a sculptor. He had dreamt of becoming a scientist, an explorer, or a great religious or revolutionary figure.

"I longed to perform great deeds. To be quite honest, I knew as a child that I would be something big, although I did not know in exactly what way. I would let the trolley car pass me by as I stood waiting for it at the stop. Then I would run after it and if I caught up with it, I would become a great man. If I did not, I would not."

During the war Neizvestny's school was moved to the safety of Samarkand and it was here that he underwent the most important part of his schooling.

Neizvestny has in his possession copies of letters that he sent home to his parents in 1942. In them, the sixteen year old boy outlines his credo.

43

Monument in honour of the Dead. Sketch. Bronze. 1970–74. (0,22 x 0,43 m).

Mask and hand. Bronze.
1959–75. (0,22 x 0,43 m).

"There is only one way for art – the path of absolute truth. Anything that is not true, is not art. There is no excuse for untruth, not even that of being young. Untruth becomes a habit. One must learn to be truthful right from the start, maybe not always openly and firmly, and never just out of cleverness. One must stick to the truth. Only this will bring me to my goal.

I can have the misfortune to be a loser in the world of art by following this path, but I can never lose out in life . . .."

*"The defenceless Life is
gobbled up". Indian ink.
1962. (0,41 x 0,51 m).*

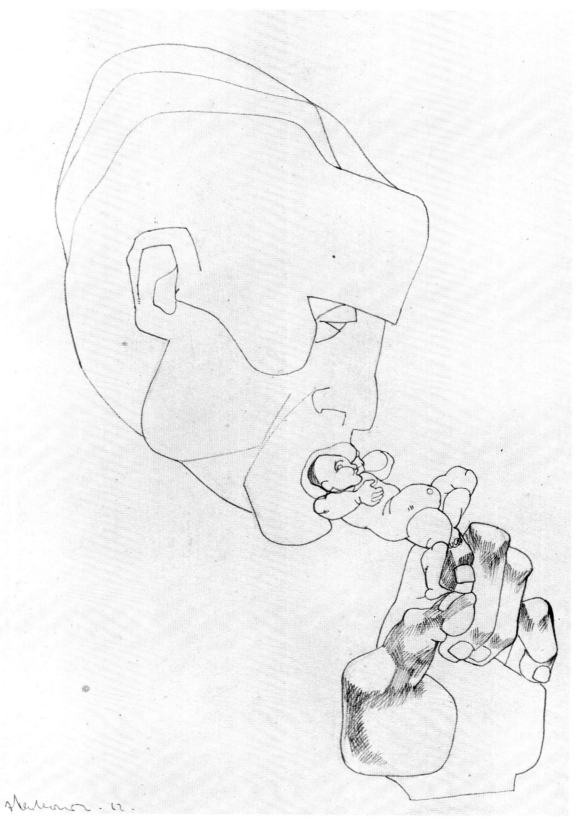

In Samarkand he went down with typhoid, developing dangerous physical and
psychical complications. He never mentioned this in his letters, in order to spare his
parents. He lost the hair from his head, went off his food, lost his memory and became
unconscious of his own identity.

But both his memory and his strength were gradually to return.

46

"Pieta". Bronze. 1976.
Modelled just before
Neizvestny left the Soviet
Union. (0,31 x 0,18 m).

War and Death

Right from the time Ernst Neizvestny came to Samarkand his intention had been to enlist for service at the front, for it was there that events of world importance were taking place.

At school he was becoming increasingly indignant. The school authorities were required to release a quota of the older pupils for military service, but a group of those who were the most proficient was to be retained. These could continue their studies.

Neizvestny saw that youngsters with influential parents were being given high grades whilst unprivileged, but more gifted pupils were marked less generously. When one of his close friends was reported killed in action after only a month at the front, he acted.

He went to the town's recruiting office, added a year to his age and joined the line of naked manhood waiting for the very perfunctory medical examination.

His hair close cropped, since he had now signed up with the Red Army, he returned to the school. Nobody could touch him now. He went straight to the headmaster's private apartment, got to see him alone and wedged the door shut with a chair. He then proceeded to beat him up in retribution for his discriminatory treatment of his pupils.

Ernst Neizvestny, at the age of seventeen, had a first class constitution. With adequate food an training he had quickly regained his health after his bout of typhoid. Since he had also volunteered, he was selected for one of the toughest officer training establishments in the Soviet Union, located in the far south near the borders with Iran and Afghanistan. Kushka, as the place was called, was a military academy known from Tsarist times.

The war situation was such that Stalin had declared a truce among ideologies and classes and, for this reason, Neizvestny's class background and the fact that he was neither a member of the Komsomol nor the Party had no effect on his selection.

The units from Kushka were specially trained for assault and landing operations. After months of hard training Neizvestny was posted to the 45th Assault Regiment, one of the units under the direct command of the C in C of the Red Army, nominally Stalin himself. The regiment was attached to the 86th Guards Division on the second Ukrainian front. Neizvestny's unit was constantly in the front line of one of the most

"Dead soldier". Bronze. 1953–54. An example of Ernst Neizvestny's anti-idealistic view of the war theme.

active sectors, that in which an army group was fighting its way from the Ukraine into east and south Europe. The regiment was used in parachute drops, sea landings and most of all, in armoured assaults. Neizvestny fought in Romania, Hungary and in Austria and was wounded several times.

"But I have no wish to retail my war experiences. There is nothing more boring than war. No romance. Writers make all that up afterwards. War is dirty. It stinks. It's full of monotonous jobs. I have written forty war poems, all of them anti-romantic.

I don't believe the officers and men who describe war as if it were something out of normal everyday life. That people have feelings for each other and that some are good and some are bad. That there is such a thing as solidarity. Who on earth can remember which guns stood where, and who moved off to the left and who to the right. I believe that accounts such as these are made up behind the lines and are the products of staff thinking.

In the front line life is a long string of trivialities. Men died so often that it was impossible to regard a unit as a collective. But maybe it was different in the war I never experienced, the trench warfare which Victor Nekrasov wrote about.

As assault and landing troops in an attacking situation we lived but for a few hours like butterflies. During training we had been told that soldiers in combat units such as ours had an average battle life of four hours.

In normal front line units war consisted of several elements and was not a continuous shooting match. Troops took up positions, exchanged fire, consolidated and then regrouped. But our special commando units were thrown into battle and got shot at whether they succeeded in reaching their objectives or not. Those who survived were withdrawn from the combat zone and rested up for two or three weeks whilst fresh units were deployed. There never was time to make any kind of personal contacts.

I fought a succession of different enemy units from 1943 until the 22nd of April 1945, only interrupted by periods in hospital. The last time I got wounded I was left for dead.

The unit I commanded as a lieutenant had just taken the little village of Heisendorf in Austria. We dug ourselves in and prepared to continue our attack. The poet Andrey Voznesensky wrote a poem thirty years later in the course of which he describes how lieutenant Neizvestny went alone to the attack. It was then discovered that the sculptor Ernst Neizvestny was that same lieutenant who had fallen, leading the attack at Heisendorf and had been awarded a posthumous medal for extreme gallantry. This caused quite a sensation at the time.

In the sector where my men were entrenched that day in April, the German barrage was so fierce that the earth shook violently. The order to attack came and I shouted it as loud as I could. The men did not as much as lift their heads under the overwhelming bombardment. I repeated the order. No reaction.

There was now no other course open to me but to repeat a third time that they were to follow me. I jumped up, ran thirty or forty yards and threw myself to the ground. I saw one soldier get up and follow me, then another, and the attack was on. The whole unit went into action. But I was hit and lost consciousness. A dum-dum bullet had entered my chest, smashed my internal organs and bones and made a crater in my back. My unit gained its objective, but I had no idea of this. I only got to hear of it when I received my medal.

I lay among a mass of dead whilst attack and counterattack surged back and forth. It was all so hectic that nobody had time to take care of those who had fallen. I was reported killed.

Later on, a stretcher party came by and found that I was not quite dead. They brought me to a field hospital knowing nothing about my having been reported killed."

What now happened was so fantastic that Neizvestny has been unwilling to talk about it, as no one would have believed him. But not so long ago his mother sent him some old correspondence from the time he was in the military hospital. This is the documentary evidence of the following facts.

The woman who washed the mortally wounded lieutenant at the field hospital, recognised some quite distinctive birth marks on his body. Among all the millions of women in the Soviet Union, this one had been Neizvestny's nursemaid in Sverdlovsk. She identified him, and took special care of him.

Neizvestny was put into plaster and suffered unceasing and unbearable pain all over his body. The doctors refused to prescribe heavy doses of pain-killing drugs. His life was at stake. But his one-time nursemaid got hold of some for him. His suffering was so intense that it became fixated in his mind with a permanent effect on the extent to which he could tolerate pain.

"One morning I woke up completely free from pain. I was at peace and content. But I could not open my eyes, could not say a word, not move a limb. I could however, hear what was going on around me.

I heard that there were doctors standing by my bed. They were saying that I was dead and gave the latin name for my condition. I had grown up in a doctor's house so I knew the terminology.

I wanted to let them know that I was alive, but could do nothing. I was completely unafraid, calm and happy.

A while ago I read a book by a doctor who had brought dead people back to life. He described the experiences of those who had died, of how they had seen a light at the end of a tunnel for example. I don't know whether there is any truth in this, but

From the Inferno series. Indian ink. Illustration for Dante's Inferno, specifically XXI Song, verses 33–36. (0,33 x 0,36 m). For Ernst Neizvestny, Dante's poetry is an unfailing source of subject matter for imaginative drawings and graphic works. He has illustrated all Dante's works with the exception of Il Paradiso. He admits to "not having been capable of grasping the mathematical musicality of the material".

E. Neizvestny. 78.

nothing like that happened to me. But that it is not frightful to die, that is true. I knew only peace and was free from pain.

The stretcher bearers came to take my body to the mortuary in the cellars, down a great many stairs. I was particularly heavy because of all the plaster. They could not be bothered to carry me so they heaved me over the banisters and went on their way. The plaster cracked open as I hit the ground at the bottom of the stairs and this presumably touched off something in my mutilated back. I began to scream with pain, I know not for how long.

In the meantime my old nursemaid had come into the ward and found my bed empty. She found out that I had died and had been taken to the mortuary. So she went down there to take her last farewell of me. And on her way down she found me lying screaming.

I was carried up again back to life and pain. But the bureaucrats had already managed to send the news of my death to my family. It was an automatic procedure.

I sent a letter from the hospital, describing what had happened. This is the letter that I now have in my New York studio.

I wrote that I believe in God. The kind of thing that happened to me just cannot be ascribed to chance.

While I was still in the Soviet Union I had started on my autobiography. When I think of what has happened to me, I have a peculiar feeling that there is someone writing the story through me. But he who is doing it has poor literary taste because there are in my life so many incredible and trite episodes which follow the most banal patterns. If for example my row with Khrushchev and the fact that I also did the monument over his grave had not been so widely known, most people would have regarded this as something only a very indifferent writer would have invented.

And what about when I was being accused in the Soviet Union of creating unpatriotic art, whilst I was at the same time the subject of a newspaper article because some bureaucrat had discovered that a certain lieutenant had been decorated with the Order of the Red Star. Everybody knows about this and takes it for granted. Much in my life has been in the same pattern.

When I came back from the war and from hospital, everything seemed so unimportant to me. For several years I measured everything with death's yardstick. It gave me strength. Gradually this attitude changed. But it is still to be found somewhere in my subconscious. And I am certain that it goes back further than to my war experiences.

I have recently been going through the drawings and the paintings from my childhood. The death theme appears in them continually. Of course my symbolic figures, the centaurs and the astronauts did not appear in my childhood pictures. They were full of masks, hands and dying persons. When I was twelve years old, I had

Crucifix motifs. From one of the "Tree of Life" albums.

done some illustrations for Dostoyevskys *Crime and Punishment*. The story of my adult life has served to strengthen my consciousness of death, not given rise to it.

My autobiography is important to me as an artist, not least because it was in my childhood that the ground was prepared for my future career. But now after some years in the West, I feel that I am in the process of losing my perspective where life is concerned. My situation has become ambivalent. In the Soviet Union I felt every day that I was being given life as a gift, and I faced the world from that standpoint. Whenever I experienced moments of happiness, and life seemed to have become easier, I would almost unconsciously supress my feeling of enjoyment in order to return to my original uncomfortable state of mind.

When I came to the West my first thought was that everything that I experienced was peanuts measured against the fact that I was alive and not in a concentration camp. I had my yardstick.

I feel that as I talk about this I am repeating my inner biography. As soon as I start to experience a feeling of comfort and stability, I turn my back in renunciation.

53

If that is difficult to understand, then it is also impossible to understand why I refused the hospitality of one of the richest families in Europe. Mr. and Mrs. Paul Sacher, who have a controlling interest in one of the world's leading pharmaceutical companies, and whose guest I was in their Basel home, had given me the run of a studio with all facilities."

Neizvestny is concerned with the difficulty of relating an artist's life to his art. He has discovered that whenever he is relatively secure and without material worries, tragedy and pain come to the forefront in his art. During a period in the Soviet Union when he was going through a particularly intense love affair, the work he did was strongly ascetic in character. Is this the pattern of the way the artist in him behaves and affects his way of life?

"I cannot do anything to affect my actions in this way. When I lived with my wealthy relatives on Park Avenue in New York, I had a cook who had been in Onassis' kitchen. I also had a chauffeur and a manservant at my disposal. But I couldn't live like that. I think it has to do with the fact that my subconscious is all the time pushing me into discomfort.

But I have the feeling that this is perhaps all over now, without really knowing how this has come about.

Now I am dreaming of getting a house of my own and living peacefully outside the big city. But I want to do this on my own. As soon as anyone starts to help me too much, the dream is shattered. Maybe I shall never be able to live as I would like. All the time I seem to be recreating an uncomfortable environment for myself.

When I drink I put my glass on the very edge of the table so that it almost falls off.

I don't know whether this has anything to do with the war, but I do know that when I am in the middle of a pleasant period, such as the one in which I am now, I start to get restless. Here in the West, I easily get bogged down in details. They seem to be important and grab a hold of you. When I realise what is happening, I break it all up in order that more important things, unhampered by detail, can take over".

"But in a comfortable environment such as that offered by your wealthy hosts you would not be bothered with a lot of oppressive detail."

True enough, but other details kept on cropping up. Questions of etiquette, correct dress, things which I previously considered trivial, suddenly became important."

"The dolce vita became an enemy of creativity, as it were?"

"No, that's not how it was. I worked well when I stayed with my rich friends in Switzerland. It was there, for example, that I did my bust of Shostakovich.

I have a wealthy friend in Miami Beach. He owns a chain of hotels. When I visit him, I get my own room with meals on the house, and I pay him with a drawing. The first time I came down I was given an especially luxurious and expensive room. I told him I did not want it and asked for a cheaper room at another hotel. My friend thought

I was afraid that it was going to cost me too much and made it quite clear that I was not going to have to pay. But I insisted on the inferior room and had to explain why.

I said that there were in that luxury room valuable objects which were foreign to me. I could not create my own atmosphere in such a room. When I come to a cheap room containing only the bare essentials, I can lay out my drawings and my books and thereby create my own world. Nothing disturbs me. The room is mine.

Even if I were to become very rich, I would have to have an austere room in which to work.

In Moscow there were times when I was very well off. I was often asked then why I continued to live in my studio in army fashion. I did in fact try to live in greater comfort, but soon discovered that I had no need to."

Our conversation turned to Arthur Koestler's observation than mankind sometimes needs to live on a tragic plane face to face with life's important questions, and sometimes on the trivial plane, an ordered, secure existence, in close contact with everyday matters. Neizvestny is preoccupied with contrasts and tensions of this kind.

"My book is concerned with just such difficulties in reconciling the heroic with the pragmatism of society. When I returned home from the front to my family and to dinner table discussions about such uncomplicated matters as where to buy sugar and how much the rent had gone up, I was almost hysterical. I fired a shot into the ceiling and shouted. How can you talk like this when millions have been killed on the battlefields?

Then I was ashamed of myself for I understood that those at home had doubtless had just as difficult a time of it as we who had been at the front. But this is the kind of thinking that has followed me all my life. When I listen to Americans talking at their coctail parties I often want to fire a gun at the ceiling."

Peace and Student Days

When peace was declared, Ernst Neizvestny, a highly decorated and badly wounded war veteran, his neck shortened after numerous operations, limped back to his old school. He had changed a great deal in looks since leaving for the front and he reckoned that everything else in the world had changed too.

But his old school, now back in Leningrad, had the same principal, the same secretary, the same notices on the notice board. Nothing, except Neizvestny, had in fact changed. Nobody recognised him. He swayed on his crutches and shouted, "Hallo, it's me, Ernst. I'm back."

An elderly woman teacher, the school's assistant Principal, took a closer look at him. All of a sudden she became hysterical and screamed out: "That ruffian has come back." People rushed up and grabbed him by the arms. He understood nothing of what was happening. He had completely forgotten the episode in which he had roughed up the Principal, his memory now full of all the terrible things that he had gone through in the intervening years. They showed him a document stating that he had been permanently expelled from the school. No other reason for this was given than his ruffianly behaviour.

He decided to pay a visit to the Principal of the Leningrad Academy of Art since the school was under his jurisdiction. He was a much-feared, convinced Stalinist. A scar ran all the way across his face, a memento of the Civil War. The young veteran demanded to know why he had not been allowed to return to the school.

"Take it easy, young man," said the old Stalinist. "They're all Jews and villains over there."

"I'm a Jew myself."

"You're no Jew, you're a hero. The liberal Jews will eat you, and me too, more than likely. You can't go back there, and there isn't, unfortunately, a place for you at the Leningrad Art Academy either. But I'll recommend you to my colleagues at the Riga Academy. They'll take you." And that is exactly what happened.

His parents thought it a most suitable solution. The professor of sculpture in Riga had been a friend of Ernst Neizvestny's wealthy grandfather before the Revolution. The Neizvestnys had relatives there too. One of his father's sisters was married to a technocrat in the upper echelons of the Soviet hierarchy. As a result of the war this man had also been appointed to a high position in the secret police. Ernst was allocated an apartment in a palatial building which was at the disposal of the state authorities.

Neizvestny had seemingly got off to an excellent start in Riga. But from another angle it was not such a good start at all. There was a great deal of anti-Soviet feeling in the Academy and when the students learned that Neizvestny lived in the building

"Aeronaut and Boy". Plaster of Paris. Student work from the early fifties.

"Foundry worker". Bronze 1962. Height 2,12 m. Ernst Neizvestny modelled this work in great haste as a demonstration after Nikita Khrushchev and his aides had accused the artist of having lost the ability to do social-realistic sculpture because of his increasing mental aberation.

reserved for Soviet government officials, and that he was, moreover, being favored by the Academy's assistant Principal, they did not take the trouble to find out who he really was, nor what kind of a background he had.

They regarded him as a typical Soviet ex-officer, a member of the breed that had occupied and stifled their country. As the only Russian in the class, he was made to feel their antipathy to the full.

Every pupil had to prepare his own clay each morning. Pieces of broken glass found their way into Neizvestny's lump of clay so that he cut his hands and arms when he started to work it. Nobody said a word to him and the students always spoke Latvian among themselves.

Neizvestny washed his cuts without a word. Despite the fact that he was a good pupil and worked well, it was a thoroughly unpleasant time for him. He was a stranger to his fellow students at the Academy and a stranger to the other occupants of the government apartments.

"I decided to leave Riga. But I couldn't tell my uncle what my real reason were. This was the Stalin era, and had I let on what had really happened, I could have triggered off a whole series of arrests of both students and teachers."

Through the agency of a government office, Neizvestny managed to transfer his apartment to a destitute young hunch-backed girl who was about to give birth to a child. Then he left for Moscow.

His departure caused a furore. Ernst's aunt's husband who had helped him get settled, was at a loss to understand what had happened. He reproached both

57

Neizvestny and his family in no uncertain terms. Ernst explained the situation to his father who understood his reaction perfectly.

The manner of his departure from Riga had some practical result many years later at the time he had his contretemps with Khrushchev in 1962 and he was in danger of losing his studio. He was unable to obtain materials and he was getting no commissions. Quite out of the blue he was invited to Riga and offered facilities there. His fellow-students from the old days had done well for themselves and now held important positions in Riga's cultural institutions.

They had come to realise how Neizvestny must have felt when he was an art student there just after the war. The young girl had told them of how he had transferred his apartment to her without payment. They had been able to work out for themselves why he had left, and they were ashamed. This was why they now came to his rescue and secured him first-rate facilities in which to work. His one-time foes became his close friends, which they still are.

In 1947 Ernst Neizvestny arrived in Moscow with nowhere to live and without a place at any of the institutes for art education. People were still starving and food rations were extremely inadequate.

Neizvestny fell ill. As a badly wounded war veteran, he was excused manual labour and was under orders to attend regular medical examinations. He also had influential relatives in Moscow, but he had had enough of the kind of help he would get from that quarter.

He managed to find himself a tiny place to sleep by taking a job as a caretaker for two sculptors. At the same time he applied for a place at the Surikov Institute, expressly undertaking not to avail himself of the facilities of the Institute's student hostel. Many applications were refused because there was no more room in the hostel and Neizvestny by this means managed to jump the queue and get into this prestigious Moscow academy.

It was a hard life. Neizvestny had to get up between four and five in the morning to stoke up the huge stoves that heated the studio with coal that he had to dig out of the ice and snow in the yard outside. Work at the Surikov Institute started at eight. What was more, the young veteran in his thirst for knowledge, made full use of his privilege of first priority in his choice of studies. In addition to art history, he chose a number of special university courses. But he was still disabled, always hungry and his muscles were flabby. This led to over-exertion and a complete breakdown. One night he slashed the arteries in his wrists.

This changed a great many things. The sculptors took him on as their assistant. He got no pay, but he no longer had to fire the stoves.

One of the Stalinist period's older, influential sculptors happened to visit these two relatively young colleagues and he noticed some of Neizvestny's work. He offered him a job as his assistant.

"Ice-hockey player". Student work in the social-realistic style.

As time went on, Neizvestny became assistant on a permanent basis to several of Moscow's best known sculptors and he started to earn money. He could now afford proper meals and he rented a tiny room of his own. During the daytime he worked at the Surikov Institute and at the University and during the evenings, and often at night and during the holidays as well, he worked with the official masters of their art.

He was registered as a student at the Surikov Institute from 1947 until 1954, one year after Stalin's death. He copied classical statues, working at the same time on his own account along the forbidden lines of Russian constructivism of the avant-garde period.

These were manifestations of form that were worlds apart. A result of the one was a female torso in marble which Neizvestny had fashioned with all the softness and sensuality of body that characterises Greek classicism. A mere art student, he had the unique experience of having this work purchased by the Tretjakov Museum.

He was forced to carry on his constructivist studies in secret. Sympathetic museum staff took the risks involved in helping him to go down into the basement storerooms where the works from this pioneer period had been hidden away.

When Khrushchev's "thaw" got under way, Neizvestny showed some of his non-figurative work, and at once became the subject of controversy. The centaur made its appearance! He had discovered a number of extreme formal contrapositions and had assimilated them into his artistic consciousness although they had not as yet found their way into his work. The struggle to achieve an individual style had begun.

He found the way both to himself and to his style in a series of anti-war sculptures;

59

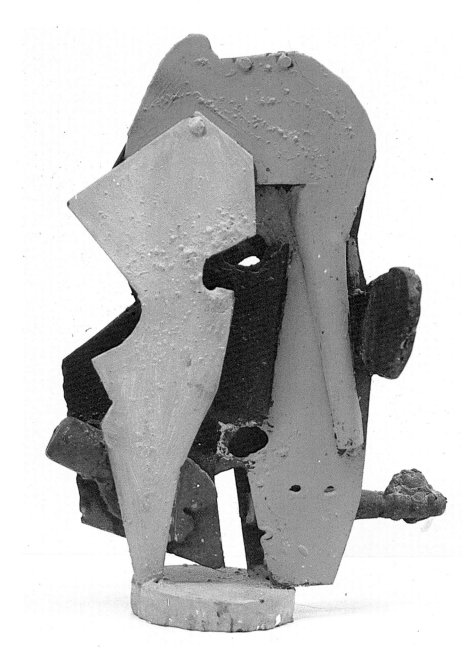

war having shown itself to him unmasked, ugly, monotonous and inhuman. After a tedious convalesence he had finally been able to discard his crutches and take up the manual labour of a sculptor. His broken back, damaged nerve tissue, mutilated liver and rib cage all started to function again. This despite the fact that he had been discharged from hospital as a total invalid dependent on medical attention for the rest of his life.

"The manner in which I regained my health might conceivably be regarded as lying outside the religious plane, although any Russian who has remained true to himself, will be inclined to see it as being religious in substance."

The will to live and life's painful victory over death and destruction was something that Neizvestny had experienced in his own embattled body. In all his trials and tribulations we see the emergence of the strength that gives momentum to his work and binds together its many contradictory elements.

"War penetrated people like a piece of metal, a foreign body," he says. War was for him a tragedy that necessitated a hard, expressionistic style. His figures of dead soldiers, walking wounded, half-suffocated faces in gas masks, roused the indignation of those artists who obediently followed the party line on heroism and popular optimism. Those of his works that were exhibited after Stalin's death, placed Neizvestny among the new generation of oppositional post-war artists of the left. After these works came robots and semi-robots and the introduction of the theme that was to recur again and again right down to the present day – the conflict between Man and mechanised civilization.

Powerful formative influences made themselves felt in his art through his studies of so-called primitive art in the museums. Especially strong was the influence upon him of American pre-Columbian art. He became acquainted with this at the great exhibition of Mexican art which came to Moscow on a European tour during the first half of the nineteen fifties and which had a section of intense power devoted to Aztec sculpture.

This was how Neizvestny released himself from the bonds of socialist realism which had dominated Soviet art throughout his time as a student.

Soviet students at that time were not, for example, given the opportunity of becoming acquainted with Picasso. The last of the western world's sculptors to be included in the curriculum was Rodin, Neizvestny recalls. This was the uncompromising result of a policy towards the arts which eliminated the last vestiges of individuality and took effect when in 1932 the Central Committee of the Communist Party "restructured" the literary and artistic organisations. The Soviet Artists Union was set up to become a powerful instrument for the ideological control of all artistic activity. Hereafter Soviet art was to seek to give "a truthful depiction of the reality of revolutionary development," as the first congress of writers held in 1934 formulated the new guidelines for socialist realism.

For years to come this parole was to result in personality cults and a tedious glorification of communist aims and of the party, the state and the proletariat. Much was done in the naturalistic salon style of the nineteeth century's popular and patriotic "Wanderer" movement in Russian painting.

The sculptors who had taken on Neizvestny as their assistant were also professors at the Surikov Institute. They were able art politicians and were mass producers of socialist realism. Gigantic statues of Stalin, the boots of which had been modelled by Neizvestny, left their studios in a steady stream. They expected that their talented young assistant would continue to work with them after he had passed his final examination at the Institute and would, as time went on, be promoted to colleague and partner.

Neizvestny says of himself that he was a well-disciplined student while he was at the Institute. His attitude to its instruction and ideas was strictly middle-of-the-road. This is as it should be, he feels. "One must get to know what one is being taught."

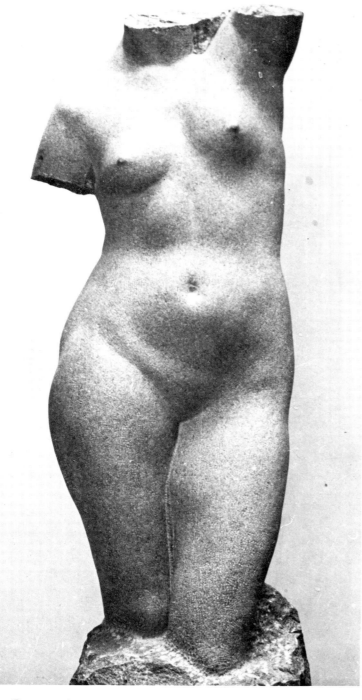

Female torso. Swedish granite. 1949. He carved this classic study when a student at the Academy at the same time as he was experimenting with the non-figurative style. This figure was later to win him a bronze medal in a competition at the 1957 Moscow International Art Festival. It was acquired by the Tretiakov Gallery in Moscow.

But at the same time, and on his own, he worked quite independently.

As time has passed and he himself has matured, his respect has grown for the academic teaching at the Soviet art institutes based as they are on German and Italian classicism.

"They give a serious and thorough schooling. Excellent for strong personalities. It has however one basic fault in that it turns the student into a professional at the same time as it takes away his independence.

I am glad that I received this schooling. But to allow it to limit my creativity, was out of the question for me. From this tension originated the state of conflict which grew up between me and my professors."

62

The Adversary accepts the Challenge

In his last year at the Surikov Institute, Ernst Neizvestny was elected a member of the Soviet Artists Union, an unusual honour for an art student. His admission to this exclusive professional group was a result of the fact that two of his works had been purchased by official museums.

Immediately afterwards, however, he popped up with his painted constructivist metal sculptures which provoked a violent reaction from his professors, especially those who were sculptors. Neizvestny was really a most ungrateful young man; one could almost call him a traitor. Had he not worked loyally and with great promise for as long as they had known him, following the official party line?

He must have gone out of his mind. And if that was not what was the matter with him, then he was nothing but a trouble-maker and an opportunist out to attract the attention and favors of foreigners.

These two insinuations continued to dog Neizvestny all through the years he worked as an artist in the Soviet Union. They were expressed in a variety of ways and in different fora; at ideological conferences where Khrushchev shouted them, at meetings of the Central Committee and the Artists Union.

He refuted the allegation that he was mad by challenging his critics to set up a committee of sculptors in the presence of which he undertook, in the space of two days, to produce a statue of a metalworker that would meet all the requirements of social realism.

He knocked up a conventional piece of sculpture without even using a model and it was so satisfactory that bronze castings of it found their way to several provincial towns in the Soviet Union.

The committee's chairman, a Lenin prizewinner, commented with no little irritation in his voice: "I was sure that Neizvestny was out of his mind. Now I can see that he is far worse. He is an adventurer."

Stalins's death gradually brought about changes, not least in the world of Soviet art. An art competition was announced, official and open to all. Designs could be submitted anonymously. This was a clear-cut break with Stalinist custom whereby the Ministry of Culture handed out commissions from the government to a closed circle of official artists. These, it was said, shared out the commissions and any other benefits among themselves.

The members of the jury were not taken from the ranks of the party careerists, but from among intellectuals in such fields as science, music and the armed forces. The main subject of the competition was a massive project for a monument to symbolise the three hundred year old union between Russia and the Ukraine.

The interest generated by the competition was sensational. Nine hundred groups of artists from all over the Soviet Union submitted designs. The way the prizes were awarded was no less of a sensation. Artists who did not belong to the official professional bodies, came out on top all along the line. A young unknown sculptor,

Vadim Sidur, won first prize. Later, and almost unnoticed, he was to become one of the Soviet Union's most interesting and consistent abstract sculptors. He expresses himself using an unaccepted cubistic form language, refined, imaginative and tragic, at times with humor. He can still only work in this way in the privacy of his basement studio, and once in a while indirectly whenever he comes into contact with collectors from abroad. Not until the nineteen seventies was he given the opportunity of executing a non-figurative decoration for a technical institute in Moscow.

Ernst Neizvestny's design also won a prize.

The relationship between the official privileged artist and the young artists with new ideas became very strained.

The art establishment tried to invalidate the jury decision by procrastinating and by putting bureaucratic obstructions in the way of those who were to build the monument.

It was a hard struggle. Neizvestny was one of the opposition. But the official art establishment was so firmly entrenched that not even the decision makers in party and state could dislodge it. The experiment with open competitions ended with a committee of official artists being given the job of overseeing the execution of the project. The prizewinners had been completely outmanoeuvered.

It was said that Sidur, the winner of the first prize, and a man of an entirely different temperament to Neizvestny, was as time went on, relieved at the outcome. The fact that he was left out in the cold, saved him from becoming an official sculptor and from the very real danger of losing both his integrity and his artistic direction.

Ernst Neizvestny's reaction was quite different. When he realised that the establishment had made away with the project and that open competition had been of no avail, he decided to break up the whole competition to punish the conspirators. He paid a visit to the person on the Central Committee who had been responsible for the competition in the first place. He pointed out that the whole affair was a political fiasco. The Party was in danger of becoming an object of ridicule. The idea of the authorities had been to build a grandiose monument in Moscow to commemorate the union with the Ukraine. But had there not been unions with all the other thirty five republics? Latvia, Georgia, Moldavia, Armenia and so forth. If the Party only raised a monument to the union with the Ukraine, the other republics would be offended. It would be necessary to mark their unions with Russia, as well. And not only in Russia, but in the Republics themselves. An inflation in monuments! And the cost would be astronomical!

The Central Committee member made no immediate comment. But he very quickly and decisively took steps to bury the whole project.

Years later the first astronaut was sent out into space. By that time there were many more artists at work in the Soviet Union. An open competition was announced for the best design for a grand monument that was to be raised to commemorate the event.

No more than a hundred artists submitted entries. All the younger, unestablished artists were convinced that even if they were to win, they would never be allowed to build the monument. The art monopoly would use its influence to ensure that the commission would go to no one outside its ranks.

"Therefore, I have to admit that the art establishment prevailed. Just before my dispute with Khrushchev I had won a competition to raise a monument to the victory over Germany. It was to be the biggest monument, not only in the Soviet Union but in the whole world, and was to be built on a hill on the outskirts of Moscow. I prepared the design together with a group of young friends and the condition was that we should build it. But after I had been censured by Khrushchev, the project was transferred to Evgenij Vychetich, the same artist who had done the monument to the Soviet soldier in Berlin.

He stole my whole idea, executed it badly and raised the monument in Stalingrad. I have photographs to prove this."

"This would seem to mean that artists are powerless to prevent their ideas being stolen from them by those who are older and well-established. Is it not possible to bring this sort of thing out into the open, and how would the authorities react to such disclosures?"

"This is where we come up against a surprising element in the Soviet psychology. It justifies itself by claiming the overriding importance of the common good, asserting that it is of greater consequense *that* creative ideas are realised than *who* realises them. In the name of this piece of ideology, official artists can exploit those who are younger. In discussions with the Minister of Culture, Furtseva, after my clash with Khrushchev, I asked her why I was not allowed to execute any commissions whilst others used my ideas and could do whatever work they liked.

She replied that I was too selfish and that I should be overjoyed to see my ideas contributing to monuments for the people."

"How did things go with you after the controversy in connection with the Russian-Ukrainian monument?"

"Up and down, mostly down. I had no studio. An uncle of mine who was an engineer and an expert on restoration work, introduced me to the director of the Novodevitche Monastery in Moscow where there was a marble statue of Christ which needed restoring after having been partly destroyed sometime during the nineteen thirties. I undertook to do the job in return for a place to work in one of the monastery towers. I worked there for a year and a half without any kind of heating."

Then Neizvestny got the chance of renting a corner of the basement of the Film Artists Union building. The ceiling there was high but there was only a little over fifty square feet of floor space to move around on; a pencil box of a room. Here he worked in stone, plaster and bronze and had to pile his works one on top of another and use a ladder whenever he wanted to look them over. He received a visit from a leading American museum curator whom the writer Yevtushenko had brought along. The American took photographs of Neizvestny's work. When Khrushchev visited the United States this same American presented Khrushchev's son-in-law Adzhubei with an album of photographs of the sculptor's work. And the question of why Neizvestny had no proper studio came up.

When Adzhubei returned to Moscow he took the matter up with the Artists Union. That was how Neizvestny came to be allocated the former beer parlour which he turned into a tiny studio, the one John Berger describes in his book and which so many international journalists have visited and written about.

It was a curious little breathing hole, with a floor area that measured no more than fifteen feet by twenty. In among the piles of drawings, prints, sketches and finished sculptures, loyal party intellectuals and bureaucrats hobnobbed with technocrats and dissident personalities. Victor Louis, the journalist and KGB collaborator, met with Amalrik, the dissident historian. Alexander Zinoviev, mathematician and writer, exchanged views with the poet Yevtushenko and independent artists such as Vadim Sidur and young Yuri Kuper. Foreigners such as Arthur Miller and Jean-Paul Sartre came here too, together with others who were less well-known such as the young Swedish provincial art-dealer Astley Nyhlén who was later to become Neizvestny's good friend and protagonist in the Nordic countries.

Neizvestny worked here at all times of the day and night. Even at night there could sometimes be as many as fifteen people in the tiny room. "Sometimes I thought to myself that it wouldn't be the KGB that put an end to me, but my friends."

The origins of this artistic environment can be traced back to the late nineteen forties when deviationist behaviour could end in liquidation. At that time Ernst Neizvestny formed a group of free-thinking people which came to be the backbone of what he called a 'catacomb culture'. Their object was to study, preserve and create whatever they could in the way of metaphysical thought.

Over the years people of different professions as well as experts in various academic disciplines took part in this work. Some left off and became high-ranking members of the communist party apparatus. They had been found useful because at a time when many scientific and academic fields were officially closed these experts were in a position to make a study of certain aspects of international social and cultural history which were of importance in a political context. Thus, when the schism between the Soviet Union and China occurred, there was an increased demand for people who could use their knowledge of traditional Chinese philosophy and culture to provide the necessary background information upon which an understanding of Chinese mentality and behaviour patterns could be built up.

"Centaur". Bronze. 1965–66.

"Machine man". Bronze. 1961–62.

"Endeavor". Bronze. 1962.

"Hermaphrodite". Zinc. 1966.

66

Others were experts on Indian affairs and on oriental religions and culture.

But work of this kind was the least important sector of the group's sphere of interest. The real need was to break down the official cultural barriers and collect information. It was thus possible for members of this underground society to read the works of Thomas Aquinas in a translation by one of their number. Likewise St. Augustin, Kierkegaard, modern existentialists such as Camus and Sartre, as well as other trend-setting young Western philosophers. Writers such as Aldous Huxley and George Orwell whose books were officially unavailable in the Russian language, were also translated and the typescript duplicated and circulated among members.

However, the main emphasis was not so much on modern philosophy and literature, but on the esoterically spiritual.

"I had grown up in an essentially intellectual home. Our library covered the philosophical and artistic renaissance which Russia experienced in the period up to 1917 with writers such as Berdyaev, Rosanov, Bely and others. I read Rudolf Steiner's anthroposophical works and knew of his first 'temple' at Dornach which burned to the ground. These schools had published numerous books of cultural value on a wide variety of subjects, among others an attempt to reconcile Dionysian rituals with those of Christianity, and an examination of the relationship between Zoroastrism and Christianity. I was familiar with subjects of this kind from my childhood and I shared my knowledge with the group in Moscow.

But fresh problems and new challenges cropped up all the time. They were part of our mission. That was why we did undercover translations of books and had them circulated. A number of those in the catacomb group themselves wrote essays and books for a circle of initiates. Fifteen such typescripts were smuggled out to the West during these years.

In all probability the KGB knew nothing about this set-up. We were very careful and it is to the credit of those of our friends who became attached to the state apparatus that they never betrayed us."

Neizvestny divides the Soviet opposition into two main categories, once again making use of the cross metaphor. Dissidents from the historian Roy Medvedev to scientists such as Andrei Sakharov, whom Neizvestny regards as a saint by reason of his way of life, function for the most part on an horizontal culture plane. They are socially extrovert. The 'catacomb culture' on the other hand is introvert, taken up with religious and spiritual questions, which is to say, vertically oriented. Both types of cultural endeavour have to face dangers of various kinds. The socially conscious dissidents tend to feel that those who are involved in 'catacomb culture' are running away from life's real problems. They are wrong about this, as Neizvestny sees it. Horizontally oriented cultural endeavour wears itself out. It needs nourishment and has long ago started to feel a need for it.

"Catacomb culture', which never in any way can come to be identified with Soviet ideology, is in jeopardy from the very fact that it has been partly assimilated into the official culture. This latter has been stripped of the means of finding its bearings by free analysis, and is for this reason basically sterile. As a result it has to be sustained to a certain extent by the catacomb culture as well as by other unofficial cultural impulses."

The most capable of the official artists gradually came to recognise that they would have withered away if some of the unofficial art had not filtered through to them. Therefore they started to introduce elements of it into their own work.

"They kept me down, but assimilated the impulses from my work even though they could not accept the thinking behind them. My friend, the folk singer Bulat Okudzhava was beyond the pale for many years. His lyrical and romantic songs had never been accepted officially, although in character they were part of the official scene. The man who made the film about the ikon painter Andrei Rublov, found himself in a similar position. Andrei Tarkovskys monumental film was not released for eight years and in the meantime his style and personal touch as a film-maker were emulated in films made by official producers. As I have already mentioned, it is perfectly in order to exploit other people's creative ideas if it is for the good of the masses.

However, the controversies were not only confined to questions of style and form. They are in fact rooted in the conflict between authoritarians with a collectivist mentality and individualists unwilling to be either controlled or manipulated. This is a struggle that is taking place all over the world, but most obviously in the Soviet Union.

The fundamental standards by which the Russian people once led their lives, and which had been engendered by the church, by tradition and by culture, were set aside and everything became barren and desolate". Such is Neizvestny's view.

"Everything is now so superficial; we need no sociological revelations. This is the secret of the novels of a Zinoviev. With the utmost clarity, he describes everything that there is to describe; nothing is hidden for there is nothing below the surface. In the West this book has been regarded as a revelation.

From the time I was quite a young lad and had visions and plans, I have been plagued and harassed by narrow-minded people. It was so in the Soviet Union and it is no different in the United States. One tends to get surrounded by people who want to draw one into petty, ill-tempered controversies.

The problem is universal, but it is dramatised in the life histories of geniuses. The point, however, is that it applies to everyone who is an individualist. A conflict arises between those who follow their inner voice and want to go their own way, and those who strive to bring everyone into line and who react against anyone who is different.

That is why the struggle is not really concerned with artistic trends and problems of style. I maintain for example, that there is no such thing as a revolutionary style. But revolutionary personalities, they exist all right. Marcel Duchamp, the Dadaist, was revolutionary. But his successors are clowns and philistines. It's the same with all the followers-on over here in the States, and it's the same in the Soviet Union although there nobody troubles to hide the fact."

On the other hand, the reaction becomes stronger and more explosive whenever the pressure from totalitarian conformity is reduced for some reason or another.

After the war, individual representatives of the new generation tried secretly and independently of each other, to develop a form language which suited their views and their experiences. Many of them had, like Ernst Neizvestny, been sucked up in the whirlwind of war just as they were about to leave childhood behind them, and had returned home as grown men. "I never had a youth," Neizvestny asserts.

During the latter part of the nineteen fifties, Neizvestny and his contemporaries on the Russian art scene experienced a springlike spell, which, unfortunately was never to turn to summer on Soviet soil. The winter had lasted from the first half of the nineteen twenties when pioneers such as Kandinsky, Pevsner and Chagall were expelled from the Soviet Union and Malevich and all the others like him lapsed into silence at home.

After Stalin's death in 1953 and Khrushchev's speech condemning his mass executions at the 20th Party Congress of 1956 including Beria's liquidation, there was a certain amount of confusion on the Soviet cultural scene. Khrushchev had not denounced the existing dogmatic cultural policies, nor had he removed any of the cultural careerists of the Stalin régime. The all-powerful quartet made up of the Ideological Section of the Central Committee, the Ministry of Culture, the Soviet Academy of Art and the Soviet Artists Union, still held the reins, although they had slackened their hold for the time being. Throughout the country, thousands of artists who earned their living in the service of socialist realism awaited developments.

From outside the loyalist establishment, noncomformist talent was filtering into key positions as jury members, contributors to art journals and artistic advisers. Some artists who had long been kept away, now obtained permission to exhibit in the art galleries. It was all seemingly a logical consequense of Khrushchev's large scale releases of political prisoners, not to mention the official rehabilitation of many discredited dissidents and deviationist intellectuals. A "left wing" group of mainly younger artists reared its head in the Moscow branch of the Artists Union. Neizvestny was one of the first to break out of the Stalinist steel eggshell and he took up a position as a leading figure of his generation.

Confirmation of the 'thaw', an epithet coined by Ilya Ehrenburg, was to be found in the tentative efforts to introduce freedom of expression in magazines and books.

Most important of all, so far as the artists were concerned, was the new régime's line calling for co-existence with the outside world. As a result the iron curtain was lifted

70

just sufficiently to form a chink. Modern contemporary art flooded in from the West. From 1956 to 1963 both Moscow and Leningrad hosted a series of important foreign exhibitions. Picasso's 75th birthday was celebrated with a fine showing of his work. There were exhibitions of Fernand Léger, of expressionistic German graphic art, of modern British, French, Belgian and American art.

The degree of interest shown by the general public can only be measured against the size of the crowds that attend the most popular football matches, as we are told in Igor Golomshtok's and Alexander Glezer's book, *Unofficial art in the Soviet Union.* Thousands stood in overnight queues to gain admission to the art galleries the following morning. Exchanges of views in front of the pictures turned into mass discussions. These sometimes ended in the arrest of the most enthusiastic protagonists of modernism, as happened at the 1957 Picasso exhibition in Leningrad. All the available information material on Western contemporary art was quickly snapped up.

A turning point for many questing Soviet artists was the Sixth International Festival of Youth in Moscow in 1957. A gigantic showing of four and a half thousand works by young artists from more than fifty countries was held in two huge pavilions that had been built in the Sokolniki Park. It was also a direct confrontation between artists from east and west. Abstract, tachistic, neo-expressionistic guests demonstrated how they worked in the special studios that were part of the exhibition.

Some of the foremost representatives of Soviet dissident art have testified to the fact that the reaction to the impact of all this experimental art, after the initial shock was over, was that here was a challenge which, if taken up, could not but lead to fruitful results.

An international competition had been arranged in connection with the Youth Festival, and Ernst Neizvestny won two prizes and should also have been awarded a third. The jury awarded him the gold medal for a granite sculpture entitled "Nature," which later came to be given as a present to Finland's President Uhro Kekkonen by Prime Minister Kosygin. He got the silver medal for a granite figure, "Mulato", and the bronze for "Torso", yet another sculpture worked in granite.

However, Neizvestny was called up before Alexander Mihajlov, the Minister of Culture, and told that it would not look at all good if one and the same person were to win all three medals. He was accordingly ordered to give up the gold medal which was promptly awarded to a friend of the Minister.

"This was symbolic of my whole life. Now and again I have been on top, very high up in fact, and at other times I have been far down. I have never enjoyed a quiet, regular existence. But I am proud of the fact that I never accepted any official positions in the Soviet system when I was at the top. If on occasions I have been seen as a leader, it was never on an official basis."

71

A Vision

The year before his triumph at the Festival of Youth, Ernst Neizvestny's fortunes had really been at a low ebb. No amount of 'thaw' could save him from the disfavor into which he had fallen. The Hungarian uprising had broken out and at this tense time the Communist Party's Central Committee accused Neizvestny of revisionism. For a time he was under suspicion of being a leader for elements sympathetic to the Hungarian cause. This political accusation was, according to Neizvestny, entirely without foundation. It was made by his enemies in the art world with the object of putting him out of action as an artist.

"Many who are interested in my career believe that my clash with Khrushchev in 1962 saw the start of my major problems in the Soviet Union. Only a few remember the campaigns against me in the press and the restrictions that were placed on me when the Red Army invaded Hungary in 1956."

The door was firmly shut on Neizvestny everywhere, and it was made very difficult for him to work.

Adversity played on his nerves. He was persecuted to such a degree that he thought it best to take himself off to Sverdlovsk.

There, he took a job as a foundry hand. On one shift he sweated away as an ordinary worker, on the other, he was allowed to cast his own sculptures out of scrap metal.

He slept little, drank a lot, and fell headlong into a state of deep depression. His hair and beard started to fall out. His work as an artist lost its meaning for him. He brooded desperately over why he worked at all. He fantasised about a time capsule, a container in which he would place his sculptures and a tape recording of his ideas and bury them somewhere in Siberia for some future generation to find.

One night he awoke with a start, and it suddenly came to him why he was a sculptor. In a flash he saw before him the "Tree of Life". He sketched a model then and there. First it was egg-shaped, a symbol of the infinite. Later on, not least for technical reasons, he came to give it the shape of a heart.

"Suddenly I wanted to live, and in this connection I must recount something of great significance for which I can only hope that people will take my word.

The truth is that I had been drinking too much in Sverdlovsk and that I had become a pathological alchoholic. But as soon as I had set my mind on doing the "Tree of Life" I decided to stop drinking. I went into a clinic for a four months cure, and when I left i didn't touch a drop for a very long time.

One night I had a dream. Expressed in words it sounds banal, but I dreamt I saw a dome placed over the world. I stood in the middle looking up at the stars. Suddenly the stars turned into eyes. I see these eyes and hear a voice coming not from outside but from inside me. I don't know whether I should repeat what it said for it was more of a feeling than anything else. But what this feeling amounted to was this: We know you. We see you. You are not alone.

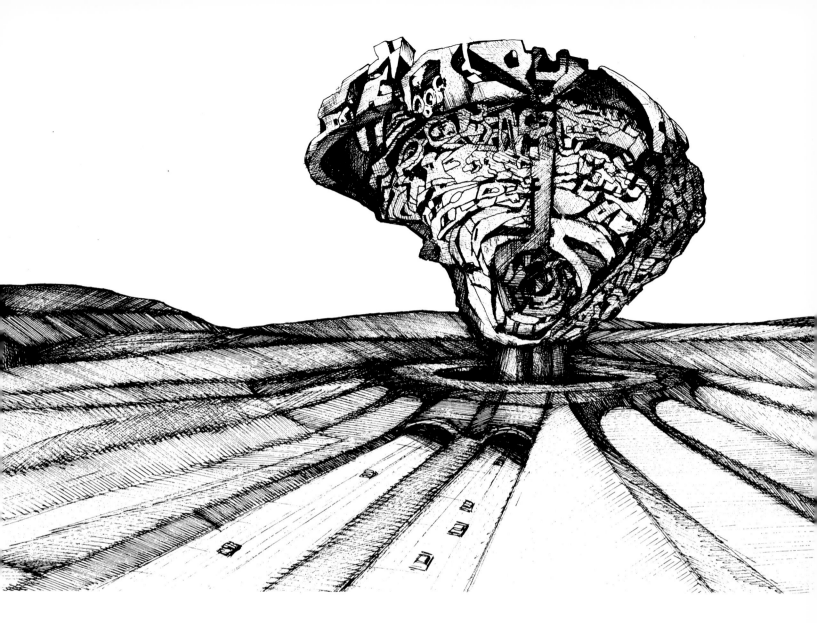

"The Tree of Life".

All these eyes radiated beams of light at me and my head grew enormously in size. It was drawn upwards, but my body remained small. My head continued to grow and I was filled with a feeling of ecstasy that is difficult to describe – a feeling, yes, of love, joy and peace. I wept and wept saying nothing but thank you, thank you. It was a very powerful experience. It could not be compared with anything I had felt before; not sexuality, not happiness. If this is what religious ecstasy is like, then I understand the ascetics.

I woke up. My pillow was wet. I was boundlessly happy. I have never been able to forget that dream.

I have consciously tried to re-create that same feeling, and it returned to me only once, not long before I left the Soviet Union. I was to take part in the unveiling of a monument I had done over those who had fallen in Northern Russia. There was a snowstorm and our plane had to put down in Vladinia. Our party was quartered in the home of a high ranking party official in the district. His wife collected ikons and she had managed to save many of these from destruction.

The evening developed into a drinking bout and I got very drunk. Our hostess said little about her collector's interest. But during the course of the evening she declared

"Shriek". Acrylics and oil. 1977–81. (1,11 x 1,73 m). The motifs are from the "Tree of Life" albums.

that she did not look upon ikons as religious art but as pictorial art of a very high esthetic standard of quality. I blew my top at this and the party left me to myself. I remained where I was in the room. Suddenly I saw that quite close to me were two beings. I don't know whether they were a hallucination or what they were, I am only describing what happened. One of these beings is obviously a woman, everything about her consists of light blue and pink phosphorescence, everything is infinitely beautiful color. Right in front of me a man is sitting in a chair, the other being. I see no face, the body is golden-brown and transparent. Two large male hands are resting on the arms of the chair. The male and female voices speak out in unison, but once again the sound comes from within me. The words are the same as in my dream: We see you, we know you, we understand you. You are not alone. But why are you so angry? You have no need to be.

Once again I experienced that same feeling of ecstasy as in my dream, though this time not so strongly. I only had time to ask: Are you the principle of the male and the female? They laughed. The rest of the party were returning and the beings said only: 'We love you,' before disappearing.

The interesting thing was that although I had been dead drunk before this

74

"Shriek". Acrylics and oil. 1977–80. The motifs are taken from the "Shriek" series (left) and from the "Strange births" series (right), both in the "Tree of Life" albums.

happened, I was stone sober when the others got back. Everyone noticed this. I was very happy. I begged the forgiveness of my hostess and the rest of the party who could not understand what had happened to me. I drank no more that night.

I don't know whether this really was a hallucination, and it doesn't matter to me whether it was or not. I believe it has something to do with a higher order of things, although I cannot of course be definite about this. I only know that both manifestations have had a considerable influence on the course of my life. More than that; I see them as being more vivid and real than the fact that we two are sitting here talking together."

"Does this mean that your metaphysical outlook on life is based on experiences of this kind?"

"I have had many such experiences, but none so vivid as these two. My outlook on life had been formed before I had them. I have quite simply a need to behave irrationally. I am nearly always being faced with a choice between two courses of action, one rational the other irrational and am drawn towards the irrational. The interesting thing is that when I go against my natural instincts and act rationally, I lose out. When I act irrationally, I succeed. I never do well using rational methods, not even in everyday matters.

75

"Mental Cry". From the album "Tree of Life". 1977–81. Acrylics and oil on canvas. 111 x 173 cm.

I once lived in a Dominican monastery in Poland – I'll tell you about that later. I went for a walk with the Prior who, by the way, had a doctorate in psychology. To the others in the monastery I had not dared to put the question which I now asked the Prior: I understand your life, your friends, your asceticism, but there is one thing I don't understand: how can you young, healthy men manage without sex?

He stopped, put his arm round my shoulders and said: 'Ernst, we are poor monks aspiring to a state of inner blessedness. You have no need to seek it for God has given it to you. The problem of sex is a vulgar technicality'."

"Did he really say that?"

"Yes he did. And when he talked of inner blessedness, I understood what he meant, because it's true. To be perfectly honest I think of death all the time whether I'm talking, eating or just moving around. The first thing I think about when I wake up is death. The last before I fall asleep. But it's not a dismal thought, it's a happy thought. It helps to relate one thing to another. It provides a yardstick against which courses of action can be measured; it puts everything into perspective. Everything becomes a pleasure, in a way rather like a game."

When Neizvestny moved from Sverdlovsk back to Moscow he was consequently in

76

"Born in Head".
1977–81. Acrylics
and oil on canvas.
111 x 173 cm.

excellent heart. The vision of the "Tree of Life" had opened for a flood of ideas and imagery. He carved the three granite sculptures which were to triumph at the Festival of Youth. But his position in the capital was still at risk. He returned home once again to Sverdlovsk in the hope that the political storm about his person would blow over.

In 1960, once again back in Moscow, he won the competition for the victory memorial mentioned earlier, with an originally conceived design. It consisted of a tunnel with the victims of war depicted on its dark walls. At the entrance, in the daylight, was a needle, tall as a building, with an inverted pyramid beside it, standing on its apex. On the obliquely slanting walls of the pyramid the names of the fallen were to be inscribed. Along these walls would run gangways for visitors, sloping diagonally downwards. At the bottom was a pool of water – a 'sea of tears'. In this lay the mask of a soldier, face upwards. The jury which favored the project had a sprinkling of generals on it, but the Soviet Academy of Art intervened and killed it stone dead.

However the project did help to bring Neizvestny to the attention of some gifted architects and this was to lead to a fruitful association in the years to come.

The next commission they could not prevent him being given. Together with his

"Shriek". Acrylics and oil.
1977–80. From the albums of
war themes.

new-found architect colleagues he had entered a competition for a monument in honor of the children of the world. Neizvestny's design was in the form of a fifteen hundred square foot basrelief which was to be set up in the town of Artek. At the same time the architects began to involve him in other major projects. Neizvestny was on his way up to the first period of success and recognition in his career.

So far he was making the most of the 'thaw', now that the accusations against him of revisionist tendencies had died away. He also managed to get himself some more elbow room in his daily working environment. For example, he was now casting several of his smaller sculptures in bronze in a home-made foundry which he had managed to construct in the yard behind the studio. This was the kind of thing that could now happen during the unpredictable, liberal period of Khrushchev's leadership.

When it came to really major projects, sculptors were and still are for that matter, the most restricted of all artists in the Soviet Union. With their need for materials and labor and by reason of the very weight and bulk of their works, they are normally totally dependent on the characteristic organisational set-up that has been developed

78

in the socialist industrial societies of the east. All artistic projects there must be executed by so-called artist combines. These are workshop collectives under the control of the powerful Soviet Artists Union. According to Soviet law, a sculptor cannot undertake a commission except through his combine. These have a monopoly of materials, technical equipment and tradesmen. Every art form has its combines, and the artists work through them according to hard and fast rules regulating how they shall participate. When an artist or group of artists is given a commission, a contract is drawn up with the combine covering all aspects of the project. It looks all very well on paper, but according to Neizvestny the system is wide open to all kinds of intrigue and manipulation.

During the latter part of the nineteen fifties and the beginning of the sixties, the number of nonconformist artists and exhibitions in Moscow and Leningrad had increased significantly. Exhibitions were now being held independently of the Artists Union in the private homes of musicians, composers and the more progressive members of the intelligentsia.

These were followed by individual shows in scientific and technical institutes and in workers clubs. Ernst showed a representative selection of his works at the Druzhba

Workers Club in Moscow in 1960. And in 1962, he exhibited at the University of Moscow together with Vladimir Yankilevsky.

At the end of that year, he also joined a formal radical group that had been got together by an art teacher by the name of Belyutin. This man had, strangely enough, obtained permission to show examples of the group's work at the Zhdanov teachers training college in Moscow. The exhibition consisted of works of an experimental nature by Belyutin's pupils, and works of his own and some of his colleagues that Neizvestny had included. The exhibition had a provocative effect and drew a very large public. After a few days the authorities closed it down.

The tension between the well-established and wealthy socialist realists from the Stalin era and the very different crowd of nonconformist artists had reached breaking point.

The former group had their citadel in the Soviet Academy of Art which had been founded in 1947. The most privileged of the traditional artists had their seat here. All the Soviet art schools were under their supervision. Furthermore they sought to direct the official art scene from their quasi-elitist academic position of strength. They met a certain amount of opposition from the Soviet Artists Union.

80

Angel and Devil

On the first of December 1962, the Moscow branch of the Soviet Artists Union was to celebrate its thirtieth anniversary. On this day the doors would open on a joint exhibition of art in the largest showroom in the capital, the Manège, a former riding school near the Kremlin. Some of the arrangements that had been planned caused much alarm among the academicians in the Union. Some of the old-timers from the early days of Modernism who had been out in the cold for so long, were to have a come-back. And the young artists of the new renaissance were also to be represented.

The Stalinist academicians laid a clever plan. The recalcitrant Belyutin group was to be encouraged to transfer its exhibition to the big official one in the Manège. There it would be inspected behind closed doors by the political leaders of the country with Prime Minister Nikita Khrushchev at their head. The academicians, together with more alert members of the general public for that matter, were fully aware of Khrushchev's emotional outbursts when confronted with nonconformist visual art. The Stalinist artists were quite sure they knew what would be the outcome of a confrontation of this kind. In his memoirs, Khrushchev wrote as follows as he takes a self-analysing backward look at the attitude to art and the cultural background that he shared with the bolshevik comrades of his youth:

"When I was serving in the political section of the 9th Kuban Army during the Civil War, I was billeted in the home of a lower middle class family. The woman of the house had a venomous tongue and she wasn't afraid of saying what she meant, 'now you communists have taken power you will trample our culture into the mud. There's no way you can appreciate a refined art form such as ballet'. She was right, we didn't know the first thing about ballet. Whenever we saw picture post cards of ballerinas we looked on them as being quite simply photographs of indecently dressed young ladies. It happened that we spoke disparagingly of Lunacharsky, the Commissar for Culture, because he spent so much money on the theater. We believed his support of the arts was the result of personal weakness and a deviation from the communist party line. But we had not yet grown up. We had come from the factories, the mines and the fields and art forms such as ballet were completely foreign to us. We have come a long way since then."

Just how long or how short a way can perhaps best be judged from an intermezzo in July of 1958 when the Prime Minister visited an American exhibition in Moscow of domestic interior decoration, contemporary household hardware and modern visual art. He became engaged in a violent discussion with some journalists and with the then Vice President of the United States, Richard Nixon, who had opened the show. Khrushchev recalls:

"Some of the objects on show had doubtless some esthetic value, but they were quite useless. And, I should add, there were some that had no esthetic qualities whatsoever. For example, there were many paintings and sculptures done in a style that the Americans regard as modern. Most of them made absolutely no impression on me. The fact is I thought them repulsive. Some of them were downright perverse. I was particularly indignant about a statue of a woman. I am simply incapable of describing how disgusting it was. It was a female monstrosity, without proportions of any kind, with a huge behind and thoroughly grotesque. I said to them (the American journalists), what would the sculptor's mother have felt had she had been able to see how her son shaped a woman? He must be abnormal or perverse in some way or other, or a pederast. No man who loves life and Nature, who loves women, could fashion a woman's body in such a manner."

Faced with authoritarian power actuated by a reactive mechanism of that kind, the Belyutin group were naturally very much in doubt as to how they should respond to the invitation. Some of the members were for transferring only the more moderate works to the Manège. But Neizvestny insisted on throwing down the gauntlet. He maintained that here at last was an opportunity to find out where the limits of authority's tolerance really lay. What was more, a tactical exercising of self-sensorship in the part of the group would immediately be detected.

They followed Neizvestny's line. The Artists worked all night to transfer their exhibits and set them up in the Manège.

The exciting moment arrived. The doors were thrown open and the mightiest man in the Soviet Union strode in, followed by an entourage of seventy; ministers, leading Party members, police chiefs, high-ranking officers.

The confrontation has become famous and there are different accounts of what happened and what the consequences were. One thing is certain; it came to mark a turning point and signalled a course of direction away from the liberalisation of working conditions for visual artists in the Soviet Union.

Khrushchev's main antagonist has so often been pestered to give his account of the clash that he has become tired of repeating it. However, Neizvestny guarantees that the following version, which is the one he gave John Berger for his book *Art and Revolution,* and reproduced in newspaper and magazine articles, is correct so far as he can remember.

Khrushchev had no sooner reached the top of the stairs than he began to shout: "Dog shit! Filth! Disgrace! Who is responsible for this? Who is the leader?"

A man stepped forward.

"Who are you?"

The voice of the man was scarcely audible. "Belyutin," he said.

"Who?" shouted Khrushchev.

Somebody in the government ranks said: "He's not the real leader. We don't want him. That's the real leader!" and pointed at Neizvestny.

Khrushchev began to shout again. But this time Neizvestny shouted back: "You may be Premier and Chairman but not here in front of my works. Here I am Premier and we shall discuss as equals."

To many of his friends this reply of Neizvestny's seemed more dangerous than Khrushchev's anger.

A minister by the side of Khrushchev: "Who are you talking to? This is the Prime Minister. As for you, we are going to have you sent to the uranium mines."

Two security men seized Neizvestny's arms. He ignored the minister and spoke straight to Khrushchev. They are both short men of about equal height.

"You are talking to a man who is perfectly capable of killing himself at any moment. Your threats mean nothing to me."

The formality of the statement made it entirely convincing.

At a sign from the same person in the entourage who had instructed the security men to seize Neizvestny's arms, they now released them.

Feeling his arms freed, Neizvestny slowly turned his back and began to walk towards his works. For a moment nobody moved. He knew that for the second time in his life he was very near to being lost. What happened next would be decisive. He continued walking, straining his ears. The artists and onlookers were absolutely silent. At last he heard heavy, slow breathing behind him. Khrushchev was following.

The two men began to argue about the works on view, often raising their voices. Neizvestny was frequently interrupted by those who had by now reassembled around the Prime Minister.

The head of the Security Police: "Look at the coat you're wearing – it's a beatnik coat."

Neizvestny: "I have been working all night preparing this exhibition. Your men wouldn't allow my wife in this morning to bring me a clean shirt. You should be ashamed of yourself, in a society which honors labor, at making such a remark."

When Neizvestny referred to the work of his artist friends, he was accused of being a homosexual. He replied by again speaking directly to Khrushchev.

"In such matters, Nikita Sergeyevich, it is awkward to bear testimony on one's own behalf. But if you could find a girl here and now – I think I should be able to show you."

Khrushchev laughed. Then, on the next occasion when Neizvestny contradicted him, he suddenly demanded: "Where do you get your bronze from?"

Neizvestny: "I steal it."

A Minister: "He's mixed up in the black market and other rackets too."

Neizvestny: "Those are very grave charges made by a government head and I demand the fullest possible investigation. Pending the results of this investigation I should like to say that I do not steal in the way that has been implied. The material I

*Ernst Neizvestny and Nikita
Khrushchev in discussion at
Khrushchev's home in 1962. From
left to right: Mikhail Suslov,
Ernst Neizvestny, Leonid
Brezhnev, Khrushchev,
Kirilenko.*

use is scrap. But, in order to go on working at all, I have to come by it illegally."

Gradually the talk between the two men became less tense. And the subject was no longer exclusively the work on view.

Khrushchev: "What do you think of the art produced under Stalin?"

Neizvestny: "I think it was rotten and the same kind of artists are still deceiving you."

Khrushchev: "The methods Stalin used were wrong, but the art itself was not."

Neizvestny: "I do not know how, as Marxists, we can think like that. The methods Stalin used served the cult of personality and this became the content of the art he allowed. Therefore the art was rotten too."

So it went on for about an hour. The room was very hot. Everyone had to remain standing. The tension was high. One or two people had fainted. Yet nobody dared to interrupt Khrushchev. The dialogue could only be brought to a close by Neizvestny. "Better wind it up now," he heard somebody in the government ranks say from behind his ear. Obediently he held out his hand to Khrushchev and said he thought that perhaps they should stop now.

The entourage moved across to the doorway on to the staircase. Khrushchev turned round: "You are the kind of man I like. But there's an angel and a devil in you," he said. "If the angel wins, we can get along together. If it's the devil who wins, we shall destroy you."

So much for John Berger's account.

Two weeks later on the seventeenth of December, a big meeting, chaired by Khrushchev, was held in the Pioneer Palace on the Lenin Heights. It was attended by four hundred delegates from the Government and Central Committee, from the art world and the intelligentsia, together with socialist realists and a few oppositional artists. In March of the following year, there was another meeting in the Kremlin's Sverdlovsk Hall with six hundred participants, where guidelines for the pursuit of the arts were also formulated.

In the meantime the mass media, the magazines, the Artists Union and the Central Committee carried out a regular witch-hunt of dissident artists and writers. The academicians' fury was directed against the nonconformist members of the Artists Union in particular. A great many artists were publicly denounced. They were responsible for deviationary artistic impulses that the authorities could keep from permeating the officially controlled institutions. But it was no longer possible to stifle them as it had been under Stalin's reign of terror. The opposition continued to function, but out of the present range of the Artists Union and the Ministry of Culture.

For Neizvestny the consequences of the slanging match in the Manège and the numerous meetings in the Central Committee were fatal. The Khrushchev régime excommunicated him.

How did Khrushchev himself see the situation on the cultural front?

"By giving his novel the title *Thaw*, Ehrenburg launched the concept which describes the period after Stalin's death," is how he puts it in his memoirs. "We who were responsible for the leadership had a positive attitude to the thaw. I too, but without mentioning Ehrenburg by name, we nevertheless felt that we had to be critical of his point of view. We were afraid, really afraid. We were afraid that the thaw would release a flood that we would not be able to control and which would drown us. How could it drown us? It could have overflowed the banks of the Soviet river building up a mighty tidal wave which would have torn away every wall and barrier in our society. From our point of view this would have been a most unfortunate development. We wished to direct the process of thaw so that it confined itself to stimulating the creative forces which would help to strengthen socialism."

Khrushchev then referred to the conferences in the Pioneer Palace and the Sverdlovsk Hall and recalls that it was Neizvestny's art that was in focus. He does not mention his threatening remarks, for example those he flung at the sculptor, and which were quoted by Harrison E. Salisbury in an introduction to Neizvestny:

"Holocaust". Acrylics and oil. From the "Shriek" series.

"The grave straightens out the hunchback." (Neizvestny is not a hunchback, but war wounds and work as a sculptor have given him powerful shoulders and a heavy musculature). The poet Yevgeny Yevtushenko, shocked at Khrushchev's crudity, responded: "Nikita Sergeyevich, we have come a long way since the time when only the grave straightened out hunchbacks. Really there are other ways." Yevtushenko's bold words touched off applause among the artists and intellectuals, and even Khrushchev joined in.

"I deplore many of the things that were said during these meetings, among them some of those I said myself," writes Khrushchev. "I remember that I criticised Neizvestny in an insulting fashion by saying that he must have chosen his name deliberately in order to remain a nonentity. I never meant that his name was suspect, but it was none the less an insult and I am sorry for it. It was unforgiveable that a person such as I, who was in a high position of state, should say anything that could be interpreted as being insulting to anyone. If I were to meet Neizvestny today (this was written shortly after his deposition in 1964) I would apologise for what I said during our discussion in the Central Committee.

Later, Neizvestny sent me a message either through J. A. Furtseva, the Minister of Culture, or through Pavlov, in Komsomol, that he would give up abstract art and concentrate on realism. I was naturally very glad to learn of this. From the newspapers, I have seen that he has done a number of excellent things and I believe that our

87

criticism may have helped to put him back on the right track, even though I deplore the form which the criticism took."

Ernst Neizvestny has the following comments to make on this account:

"At our first meeting, Khrushchev came with the now well-known statement that he saw both an angel and a devil in me. In the course of the remaining two years he was in power, he tried to eliminate what he saw as being the devil in me. And it was no metaphor. When I once asked the Party's chief ideologist in Moscow, Yagodkin, why he persisted in terrorising and persecuting me, he replied: "We are driving the devil out of you.""

"I was called in to a whole series of ideological meetings in the Central Committee, where I was violently criticised, also by Khrushchev himself. He accused me among other things of having been the leader for a Moscow group of Hungarian oppositionists from 1956. This was the old revisionist story which somebody had whispered in his ear.

Lebedev, Khrushchev's right hand man and secretary, called me in to see him at least twenty times. He was the man who had prepared the ground for the appearance on Khrushchev's desk of Solzhenitsyn's novel of the forced labour camps, *A Day in the Life of Ivan Denisovich.*

Lebedev insisted that I write a letter to Khrushchev, mentioning how much I admired him and saying that his criticism had helped me in my work.

The reason why Lebedev was so adamant about this was that a campaign had been instituted to bring oppositional dissident intellectuals back under the Party's control.

I was one of the targets of the campaign, and among others they had in their sights, were the writers Yevtushenko and Voznesensky.

I wrote a letter, but it could just as well have been written for publication in the West, since all I did was to set out my views on art. I heard through Lebedev that Khrushchev had read my letter with interest. However, the ideological section of the Central Committee had not been satisfied. Lebedev, differentiating here between Khrushchev and the Central Committee, repeated that I would have to put in writing that Khrushchev's criticism had been helpful to me. There were humorous episodes. Lebedev said: "Can't you sit down here and now and write the letter in your own hand and be done with it?"

I passed this suggestion off with a remark about my not being able to spell very well.

"That doesn't matter at all," answered Lebedev, "Khrushchev can't spell either."
"When they didn't get the letter they wanted, they started to maintain at closed Party meetings that I was in fact contrite. This is what Furtseva, the minister of Culture, or Pavlov must have reported to Khrushchev. But it would have been naive to believe this. Had I really wished to show remorse, I would have informed Khrushchev directly and without delay.

Once while Khrushchev was visiting Yugoslavia, Lebedev rang me almost daily. Ernst, he said. Why can't you see the error of your ways? Khrushchev can't sleep nights because of you. You really must try and gratify the old man now.

The rumors that the Party had been spreading, also reached my father. Once when I visited him he said to me: I used to be proud of you. But now party members are saying that you have come over to them and have confessed your guilt.

I answered: "They are not interested in confessions made in secret. If I had said A, they would immediately have followed up with the rest of the alphabet in a blaze of publisity. Have you in fact read about this anywhere?"

The significance that the Soviet leadership attaches to deviationist art, is in strange contrast to the pragmatism of their power politics and to their materialistic way of thinking, an example of which is Stalin's sneeringly ironical remark made during the war: How many divisions has the Pope?

Where is the explanation for this to be found?

The Soviet powers-that-be look upon the artist as something more than a craftsman, and for this reason are afraid of art. That's why they treat everything that is drawn or painted so seriously. There is, maintains Neizvestny, something subconsciously oriental about the idea that art is more than just the beautification of life.

"The concept of identification is a profoundly heathen idea. It goes back to the time when the hunter made a drawing of a hunt in which a mammoth was killed. This was a preparation, a powerful magic ritual to be performed before the killing took place.

In the same way, Soviet leaders believe that if a hero is depicted, then everyone will be a hero. Depict a strong man and everybody will be strong. A parody of course, but one which embodies a metaphysical relationship to art that has been lost in the West. For this reason the artist is taken so seriously that they keep him locked up as they did in olden times. Phidias was imprisoned after he had drawn his own face on a goddess' shield. The mandala, the ikon and the temple are characterised by a spiritual dimension. To the Soviet authorities a painting is something more than a work of art."

When Khrushchev was toppled, Neizvestny got to hear of it before the news was published. He tried to get in touch with him over the telephone through Lebedev, to whom he said the following:

"For two years you have been insisting that I make a public declaration that I respected Khrushchev. Now I can tell you what I really think about the matter, and you can be quite sure that our conversation is official."

"He laughed for we both knew that the line was tapped by the KGB:

'I can tell you that I had a very great respect for Khrushchev because he freed so many people, and because he exposed Stalin's misdeeds. Compared to this I do not consider that our controversy about style had any essential importance. I ask you to convey my greetings to Khrushchev and to tell him that I wish him a long life and good health.'

Lebedev replied: 'I had expected nothing else from you.'

Two months later this relatively young man was dead. He had fallen ill quite unexpectedly; a strange story. But he had found the time to repeat his conversation with me to Khrushchev. It is said that the old man had burst into tears.

I assume that it was because of what I had said, that Nikita Khrushchev invited me three times to visit with him at his house in the country. The invitations were conveyed to me by the artist, Zhutovsky, who is to-day married to Khrushchev's grand-daughter.

I did not follow up these invitations, but it was not because I was afraid to do so. After my telephone conversations with Lebedev, a KGB agent had visited me in my studio.

'We do not understand you?' he said. 'We know what you said to Lebedev over the telephone. Why must you keep on ruining your career?'

My answer to him was not exactly polite: 'A prerequirement for being able to understand me is that one is not a eunuch.'

Somewhere in what I have just recounted, is to be found the origins of Khrushchev's idea that I should do his tombstone. The fact that I carried out his wish can also have diminished whatever hopes I ever had of staging a comeback in my career.

High-ranking Party officials had hinted more than once that it would do me a lot of good if I were to identify myself with the campaign against Khrushchev. But I refused, for exactly the same reason as that which made me refuse to write that deferential letter to Khrushchev while he was in power. I had quite honestly tried to get myself to do it, but the words just would not come. It wasn't only Lebedev who pestered me; others such as Yevtushenko often stopped by and pleaded with me – he himself had capitulated. He offered to formulate the letter for me so that all I had to do was sign. Even Dimitri Shostakovich, the composer, told me that I was behaving stupidly – the most important was for me to continue my work as a sculptor. He once said in a fit of irritation: 'Don't you realise what sort of a system we are living under, Ernst?'

I believe that what saved me was my sense of style, or rather: inside me sat a naughty boy who wouldn't give in, although my better judgement told me that I should adapt. This is the reason why I was persecuted even after Khrushchev's fall – right up until 1969.

As a curiosity, I should mention a bet I made with two of my friends, the writers Maximow and Zinoviev. Both maintained that I ought to get out of the Soviet Union since all doors were now closed to me. Zinoviev was quite convinced that there was absolutely no chance of my being permitted to do Khrushchev's tombstone.

Neizvestny with one of the many visitors to his Moscow studio, Sergei Khrushchev, son of the Chief of State and Party leader.

I was sure that not only would I do it, but that I would also become the wealthiest sculptor in the Soviet Union and the one with major commissions. This was in fact how it turned out. Maximov can vouch for the bet. It was the first thing that we talked about when we met years later in the West."

However, before all this happened, the rebellious Neizvestny was expelled from the Artists Union, and was in danger of losing his studio. He was never told the real reason for his expulsion, the official reasons being that he had behaved improperly, drank too much, adopted an uncivil attitude to the authorities and scorned collective work. But not, however, for having gainsaid Khrushchev. He was ostracised as if he were a dubious character. Official assignments and facilities for working were taken from him.

It was at this time that his former enemies from Riga came to his rescue. In Riga, he was able to continue his work on the Artek monument more or less under ground, at any rate so far as Moscow was concerned. Officially, nobody there wanted to know.

Strength through Adversity

The years of disfavor from 1962 to 1969 were hard ones for Ernst Neizvestny and for many with him. The Soviet cultural climate underwent a cooling down period marked by the trials in 1965 of the writers Daniel and Sinyavsky, both of whom were sentenced to long spells in forced labour camps for having published books in the West. The Brezhnev era was under way, with its insidious rehabilitation of Stalin and its more subtle, but none the less effective methods of repression.

In addition to the breathing space he had been given in Riga, Neizvestny was occupied during these years on projects where his friends among the architects could use him anonymously, among them a project which won a Lenin prize. And then he drew a great deal. The grand series of illustrations of Dante's and Dostoyevsky's works saw the light of day – themes which had fascinated Neizvestny since his childhood.

The pick of the Dostoyevsky drawings came out as a distinguished example of the book illustrators art in a work that was later to be published as an anniversary edition.

It was at this time that Neizvestny seriously went in for graphic art, and this resulted in a prodigious and spontaneous production of drypoint etchings.

Looking back, it seems that this period of repression merely served to stimulate his creative and imaginative powers. Plagued and distracted as he was by official artists and political agencies, he managed to model several of his best known works. The semi-abstract sculpture "Endeavor", the works "Orpheus" and "The Prophet" were all fashioned in clay in 1962. The latter was not cast in bronze until 1969. Several of his most powerful crucifixes and centaur figures were created in the mid sixties, among them that in which a human torso with arm uplifted, stretches out from within an animal's solid and rounded form. The sculptural gigantomachia triptych which he regards as one of his most important works, was begun in 1962 and he worked on it until well into the seventies. Both in the series of prints and the group of sculptures with the same title, we find a theme, which, according to Neizvestny, is inspired by Scopa's world of hellenic sculpture in the altar of Pergamon, depicting gods and giants joining battle. Neizvestny sees it as the battle between robots and human beings that is innate in our time.

He began working on the albums for the "Tree of Life" in 1965. The plastic model of the project was begun in 1968 and was cast in bronze in 1976.

Neizvestny kept himself going financially by selling works under the counter so to speak, not least to foreign visitors, and by taking on extra jobs, anonymously, for official architects. His fearless, creative spirit made an overwhelming impression on people. No amount of disfavor could keep it down. John Berger's visit came at this time and his book bears witness to the way the artist overcame adversity.

And then, one day in 1969, Neizvestny heard of a competition that was about to be held under the patronage of President Nasser of Egypt, for a monument close to the

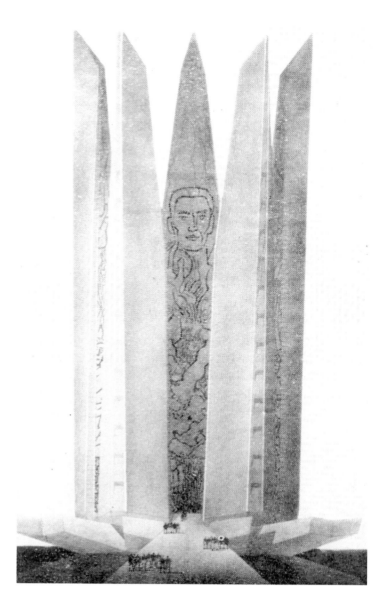

Aswan High Dam. As the Russians saw it, the monument would symbolise Soviet-Egyptian relations with dimensions that would make it the largest in the world. The Egyptians on the other hand wanted it to commemorate the building of the huge hydro-electric facility at the head of the Nile. An international jury would ajudicate the entries.

The project was still unbeknown to the main body of Soviet artists, probably because the authorities had planned to restrict participation to selected artists, loyal to the régime.

But Ernst Neizvestny had in all secrecy developed his own design, based on the conception of the lotus flower which is a symbol of friendship in the Orient. He envisaged leaf formations rising upwards in gothic style to a height of two hundred and seventy feet. He added a gigantic relief with motifs from the "Tree of Life".

He brought in two young architects to assist him with the construction side of the project. He smuggled the finished designs out of the country with the help of influential friends who were allowed to travel abroad. His confidence was such that he could say to them: If no more than one lotus design concept is submitted, we will win.

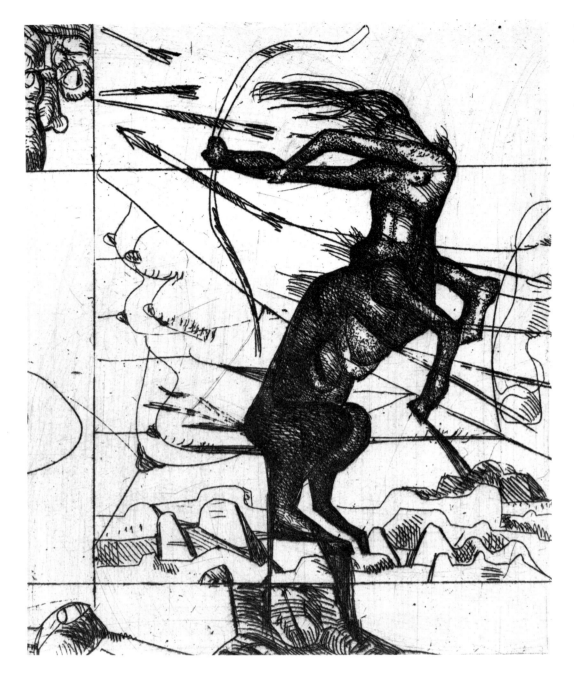

Etching from the "Fate" series. 1974–76. This series consists og 365 prints and represents what is in effect Neizvestny's spontaneous pictorial diary. This print has been exhibited among other places in the Dutch Stedelijk Museum, in the Musée de l'Art Moderne in Paris, and the Lincoln Center in New York.

Journalists and the jury members from the Western countries were present when the envelopes containing the jury votes were opened in Cairo. The news of Neizvestny's winning design was made public in both the Western and the Soviet press. This success forced Neizvestny back into the limelight of the official Soviet art scene, from the wings right on to the very center of the stage. He was offered the responsibility for the esthetic planning of four whole townships, new, closed military communities located in the north of the country.

Neizvestny sets no great store by the Aswan monument, except for the way in which his success became a jumping-off ground for future possibilities.

He was given the opportunity of paying a visit to Egypt and to study the art and architecture of this ancient land of the Nile. The impressions he gained were lasting and served to reinforce his artistic intent. However he was not able to do the relief as

"Orpheus". Zinc. 1962–64. (1,32 x 1 m). This work was started the very same day the artist had his fateful and dramatic exchange of views with Nikita Khrushchev in the Manège in Moscow in 1962.

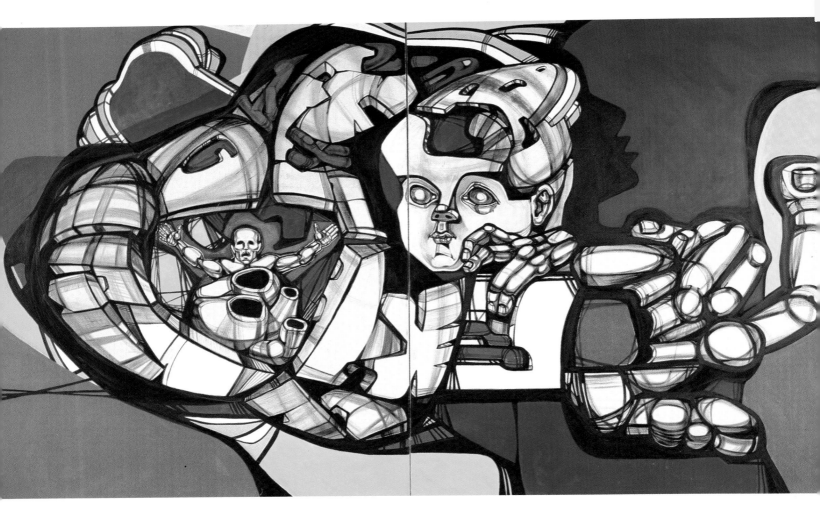

"A child's heart". Acrylics and oil. 1979–80. (4 x 2 m). This motif has also been executed as an etching.

he had planned it, using themes from the "Tree of Life". The Soviet art authorities put a stopper to that idea.

He was, nevertheless, offered back his membership of the Artists Union, not because of his Aswan success, but so far as Neizvestny recollects, as a belated result of the Heisendorf episode during the war. It had come to light that the badly wounded commando officer was none other than the controversial sculptor. He was, thus, a person who had been found deserving of one of his country's very highest military decorations. This information was published in the magazine Yonost in 1965, accompanied by a long piece of verse about the episode, written by the poet Voznesensky and which he later published in one of his volumes of collected verse.

The leaders of the Artists Union could not believe that this could have happened purely by chance. It had to be a signal from the political leadership. It seemed that they wanted the black sheep back in the fold.

But first he had to write a letter asking forgiveness. Neizvestny refused. The Central Committee called him in and made it clear that demonstrations of this kind were no longer necessary. And he got his membership card back.

Э.Н.68

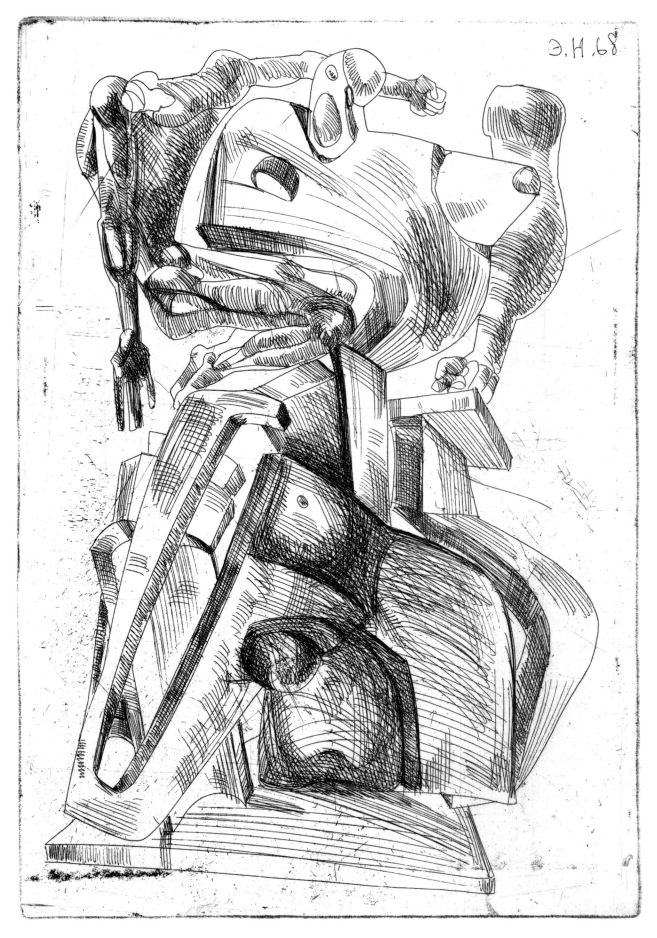

"Gigantomachia".
Left, a fragment.
(0,92 x 0,71 m).
Right, the work in its entirety,
started in 1962, completed in
Sweden in 1977.

Years of Success

Neither Ernst Neizvestny's rehabilitation, nor his Aswan monument provide an adequate explanation of the complete reversal of his fortunes and of why he was given so many important commissions during the course of the next five years.

The explanation is to be found in Neizvestny's collaboration with young, go-ahead architects and a generations of technocrats, all of whom had reached positions of authority. What had in fact taken place was that these people had broken away from Stalinist pseudo-classicism and now sought forms of building design, town planning and decorative art that were more in keeping with the times. Some architects had tried to rekindle the constructivist fires of the nineteen twenties, others were preoccupied with modern ideas from the West. The form and whole appearance of a building were often determined in collaboration with the sculptor, recalls Neizvestny.

It is not so strange that Neizvestny should have been so much sought after and was given the big assignments. Right from the time Modernism had its breakthrough in Russia, the sculptors had been left behind. This pioneer period was first and foremost a product of the efforts of the painters and of the artistic talent that was oriented towards industrial technology.

Now, with the changed signals of the post-Stalin era, the situation was repeating itself. The sculptors of Soviet realism had in general no feeling for, no means of giving expression to, the new requirements of building design and town planning. But Neizvestny, with his flexible synthesis-oriented receptiveness of both mind and formal expression, his extroverted and sweeping imagination which so easily captured the essence of both project and zeitgeist, and not least his practical sense about which we shall shortly be hearing, must have been a most stimulating partner at this time of change. He and his collaborators among the architects were supported by powerful Soviet technocrats who were feeling the need for change. Neizvestny mentions examples such as Shockin, the Minister for the Electronics Industry, Neporozhny, the Minister for Hydroelectric Development, and Antonov, the Minister for Electrification. There were also a number of leading scientists and Party officials. This circle of technocrats was made up of men who were colleagues of Prime Minister Kosygin, and some were also his personal friends.

They used the transition to a new architecture to give Ernst Neizvestny assignments in defiance of the wishes of the Ministry of Culture, the Academy of Art, and the Artists Union. It became impossible for Neizvestny's traditional antagonists to make any direct protestations against the decisions of the Kosygin group. But intrigues against him were rife.

Neizvestny more than once got the better of them with the help of the new methods he had developed for constructing his monuments. These methods also brought him in a great deal of money. Most important for him however, was that they enabled him to act unexpectedly and to catch the leaders of the Artists Union and the watch dogs of the Central Committee off their guard.

100

Plastic relief in the Institute of Electronics in Moscow. 1974. (970 m²)

With a view to one day being able to realise the "Tree of Life", he had been forced to think out the most effective industrial methods for carrying out this immense project within a reasonable space of time.

Conventional practice in the Soviet Union decreed that the first that had to be done was to make a model of any monument that was to be built. It was then enlarged as a plaster cast. This was corrected and then approved by representatives from the government or other official body that had commissioned the work. The plaster model was then enlarged further, corrected and approved once again, and so on until the projected format was attained and the work ready to be executed in its final material, stone, bronze or whatever.

"Why use such outdated methods?".

"Because the constructivist school had been killed off in the Soviet Union. Russian sculptors were for the most part drawing-room sculptors. They could not envisage a large scale sculpture first time round. They did not have sufficient spatial perception," asserts Neizvestny.

"I had no need of these initial phases. I could envisage a model on its full monumental scale. When I made a sketch I did not need to modify it when it was enlarged. It was an exact mini-replica of the final version. Although I am no constructivist in the real sense, I used constructivist elements in my work. With the help of the principles of three-dimensional mathematics in a system of co-ordinates

101

not new in itself, together with specialist collaborators and streamlined technical methods, I could complete a work on its final scale in a hitherto unheard of tempo.

An example of this was my commission to decorate the new building of the Institute of Technology and Electronics in Moscow. It ended up as a nine thousand square foot, non-figurative, clean-lined composition.

There had been a three year battle over this relief, and the delays and other difficulties had been created systematically. With only six months to go before the inauguration of the building, I got the green light to go ahead from the Artists Union, which had been under pressure from Shockin, the Minister of the department involved who was backed by Prime Minister Kosygin himself. My enemies were convinced that it would be out of the question for me to get this gigantic relief finished within the six months that were left. Thus was the trap set. I had accepted the commission and taken the money to carry it out. The whole Central Committee was going to attend the inauguration ceremony. If I failed, there would be a scandal.

My opponents were overjoyed that, in spite of everything, I had undertaken in writing to have the work finished on time.

I placed an order for clay.

There was no clay, came the reply.

Can you imagine it! Nowhere in the whole of the Soviet Union was there clay to be had. It was winter, and the message was that the clay deposits near Leningrad were frozen solid. All right, I said. We'll work in plaster. The next thing I was told was that there was no room available for me to work. I managed to arrange for permission from the building authorities to work on the site of the building on which the relief was to be put up. But the building was unfinished, and it was, as I have said, winter. In the judgement of the Moscow sculptor combine there was no possibility for me to get anything done and for this reason I had not been allocated any craftsmen for the job. I didn't need any, however.

No outsiders knew that I had handpicked my own group of assistants over the last ten years. I had always adopted the policy of ensuring that they, in addition to being sculptors, should also be able to work as masons, carpenters, plasterers, electricians and the like. In reality I had my own little firm. My assistants worked without pay, but we had an arrangement whereby they got a sizeable share of the money I was paid for the big commissions.

Usually these monies go to the artist's combine which is responsible for producing the monument in question. This time, however, I had said that I was not going to bother the combine. I undertook to execute the relief on my own responsibility. The combine washed its hands of the project and was indeed happy to do so. Nobody could see the combine, even if it were to use every man it had at its disposal, actually being able to complete the job in such a short space of time.

Stone relief at Artek in the Crimea. Monument in honor of all the world's children. 1966. (150 m²)

My assistants and I skipped all the intermediate stages and, using our own special technique, executed the relief in its final form directly on to the wall of the building. And as an extra, we decorated three other walls which were not included in the project.

A week before the inauguration I invited the official jury to come and inspect the relief.

The commission set off, convinced that the work was unfinished. On the coach on the way to the site, I had the feeling that they were almost sorry for me, and felt concern for me, the loser.

When they entered the building, they could see at a glance that the relief was up there on the wall, an exact replica of the model they had approved.

There was a deathly hush.

"Well, do you give your approval?"

"What else can we do?," mumbled the commission's chairman, quite taken aback. Preparations for the ceremony were going on all round them; carpets were being laid, chairs brought in, and the positions of floral arrangements marked out.

I had something to say to them:

'I have not done this relief for money, but to demonstrate that I could carry out the project. And now I will show you my personal gift to the Nation', I continued, and pionted out that the relief was not the 900 square foot decoration that had been commissioned but one that measured 3000 square feet."

103

Neizvestny and his assistants had made over 2000 square feet of relief free of charge in that they had decorated three walls in addition to the original long wall. This they had done because the architects had asked them to.

"What did the commission say to that?"

"Its members gave me the gratest compliment I have ever been given in my life. They wandered about the hall in silence. The chairman slackened his pace and came up to me. "Ernst," he said, "I have always wondered whether Michelangelo's awe-inspiring genius was divine or demonic. I don't know whether you are divine or demonic, but you are certainly awe-inspiring."

He turned on his heel and left.

I learned through my own sources of information that he had later held a special meeting of the commission. They had agreed that I must be put in my place. If I were to be allowed to have a free rein I would become the most important figure in Soviet art. This would create big problems for the union. If I were to continue to work in this manner I would upset the whole art scene.

However, since I could undertake commissions independently of them, there was little they could do for the time being.

But I knew they would get to me in the end. They were for example perfectly capable of getting a law passed that would prohibit the kind of work I was doing, since this had created a precedent which threatened their position.

I found no pleasure in my triumph. I am no gambler. All I want is to work in peace. I find it tragic to think of all the energy I have wasted on nonsense of this kind for nearly two-thirds of my life. This is the real reason why I ended up leaving the Soviet Union. I came to realise that I just did not have sufficient strength to tilt ceaselessly at such windmills."

One day in the early seventies when Neizvestny had the wind from the technocrats in his sails, a commission arrived from Antonev, the Minister in charge of the Department of Electrification.

The Minister wanted something to symbolise the technology which was to be featured at an exhibition to be held in the Skolniki Park to mark a particular milestone in the history of electrification. The work was to be set up under the dome which an American architect by the name of Fuller had built for an American exhibition that had been held there some time back.

At the center of the arrangement Neizvestny planned to erect a fifty foot high mobile, a baroque torso of Prometheus with light between his hands. About him would be a garden of trees made up of multi-colored neon tubes, together with a series of stands arranged in the form of a spiral. The lighting arrangements were to be programmed in such a way that when the current was switched on, light would shoot through the torso and multi-colored light would spread out through the trees and

Relief of the facade of the communist party headquarters in Ashkhabad, capital of Turkmanistan. 1974–75. The huge stylised face is cross-like in form and this became obvious in full-scale. Those who had commissioned the work were greatly displeased.

104

stands. The symbolism could not be better, was Antonev's opinion. But one of Neizvestny's steadfast antagonists, Yagodkin, Moscow's chief ideologist, made it very clear that the sculpture would only be set up over his dead body.

There were twenty days to go. The model was finished, in wax. Neizvestny now placed a metal rod in the middle of it. Several points were made to emanate from this axis like light bearing rays. Thereupon he melted the wax so that only the metallic point arrangement was left. The plaster sculpture was then clad with a light, elastic skin of aluminium. The plaster was then removed and the aluminium statue that remained was cut up into sections, ready to be moved to the site under Fuller's dome.

"But how are we to get the sculpture set up in defiance of the veto? I am a communist too", said Antonev the technocrat, his innermost thoughts scorning questions of ideology.

Neizvestny's plan of campaign was to have all the showcases and stands, the spiral and all the costly electronic equipment installed first. Nobody knew that the sculpture was ready and only wanted setting up.

"We shall surprise them", said Neizvestny. "During the last twenty four hours while the installation work is being completed we will wire up the sculpture and erect it. Then it will be obvious to everyone that the whole exhibition will be ruined if the sculpture is taken away.

The chief ideologist arrived. Minister Antonev kept away and sent his second-in-command.

"The sculpture has been set up after all. It's an ideological deviation", snarled Yagodkin. "I said this would happen over my dead body. Get rid of it at once".

"Sorry. But you'll have to die then, comrade Yagodkin", replied the sculptor.

The Vice-Minister for Electrification declared in rather more diplomatic terms that he apologised for the fact that his Ministry was not strictly in accord with ideological guide-lines. He also made it quite clear that the sculpture could not be removed without at the same time dismantling the electronic equipment which had cost them a very large sum of money.

The chief ideologist raged, but to no avail.

There was no doubt but that the "irrational" sculptor with his modern, imaginative way of thinking, had the support of the technocrats and the architects. He was given several other commissions to "mise en scéne" technical exhibitions.

His biggest commission, a gigantic one for a sculptor, was to take the responsibility for the overall beautification of four new closed military communities in Siberia from both the environmental and the town-planning angles. However before he could be allowed to undertake this work, he would have to sign an agreement not to divulge state secrets. He refused, because it would have prevented him from getting an exit permit. By that time Ernst Neizvestny had come to realise that he would have to get away from the Soviet Union.

106

In the long run it did not help him that all through his creative career he had enjoyed the support of the technocrats. His first modest independent exhibition was held at the Kurchatov Atomic Research Institute. Among those who helped him was the Nobel prizewinner in theoretical physics, Leo Landau, whose memorial stone he was to make. The academician, Pjotr Kapitsa was a close friend. Sergei Korolev, the man who designed the first Soviet space satellite, supported him.

How was it that Neizvestny came to receive so much support from scientists and technocrats?

"It is a complicated story. Now, I had never disguised my lack of enthusiasm for the technocratic mentality. These people are the best educated in the Soviet Union. A few like Sakharov are dissidents. Their way of thinking is altogether more cultural than ideological. The technocrats are better informed than the ideologists, maybe for intellectual reasons, maybe for others. They are essential to the development of the Soviet society, and for this reason they can allow themselves a certain amount of noncompliance."

"Maybe they recognize the need that creative processes have for a certain amount of freedom?"

"That's a difficult question. I believe there is an element of snobbishness in the way they behave. But it is quite clear that the sober, practical sensibility of the technocrat has a need to be exposed to modern trends and styles in the arts and the environment, something for which the ideologist has no need. At all events, the technocrats have helped me a great deal.

When I speak of technocrats, I am not only thinking of those who are employed in the official technological institutions. A number of technocrats in the KGB and on the Central Committee have shown me greater understanding than the ideologists, even though they did not help me directly".

Neizvestny's Meeting with Poland

Ernst Neizvestny, the favorite of the technocrats, was also accepted by those of the Christian faith.

In 1973 he was invited to visit Poland by leading Polish communists who had read his observations on synthesis in art. His principal hosts were Miezystaw Rakovski and his wife. Rakovski was to achieve notoriety as vice-premier during the period of martial law in 1981–83 as a tool of Soviet interests. The meeting with Poland was an important event in Neizvestny's life and he often returns to the subject of his experiences there.

He also came into contact with Catholic circles there as a result of an account of an interview with him in Moscow, written by the editor of a Polish Catholic journal.

The communist authorities held a grand reception for him in Warsaw. He also travelled to Krakow. While he was at the hotel there he was invited to visit the 12th century St. Yacek monastery by one of the monks, Father Andrej. Neizvestny accepted at once. As a Soviet citizen he should as a matter of course have consulted the Soviet Embassy or Consulate before doing so. He did not, convinced of the fact that he would have been refused permission.

"When I arrived, I discovered that some of my works were displayed in the monastery. I was shown round the whole of this ecclesiastical establishment which was set out in the following way: first we passed through a section that was open to everybody, then through halls which were used as a Catholic youth club, and this was where my works were being exhibited. From there we went into the part of the building where the novices lived. Then we came to a very old door over which hung a large cross. Father Andrei told me that I was about to be the first layman and person who was not a monk to be allowed to enter the area beyond the door.

I asked the reason for this and was given the answer that they respected me. My crucifix was in the Pope's collection. This is true, but I have no idea how it got there. It had been bought by some Italians who had visited my Moscow studio, and is now on permanent display in the Vatican Museum's department of modern ecclesiastical art.

I took a chance on a joke outside this ancient door. Father Andrei was carrying my big old-fashioned cuitcase:

"Do you know what kind of a suitcase you are carrying?"

"It is yours is it not?"

"No, it belongs to Khrushchev."

He almost let go his hold.

The fact of the matter was that when I was getting ready to leave for Poland, I could not find any case suitable for carrying the packet of drawings that I wanted to take with me. Khrushchev's son Sergei heard of this and lent me one of his father's old suitcases, to which was affixed a copper plate with his name on it.

We passed down a long corridor with tiny cells on each side. The sound of

"Heart of Christ."
Bronze. 1973.
62 x 41 cm.

108

Crucifix. Part of the "Gigantomachia" work. 1962–77. (0,83 x 0,80 m).

"The Crucifix of Mankind". Bronze. 1974. (0,70 x 0,35 m).

typewriters came from all of them. Dominicans such as those in this monastery were the most intellectual members of the Polish Catholic church. They all had high academic degrees and mastered several languages. Many spoke Russian.

I was shown to an ascetic cell. It consisted of a bunk with a hard pillow, worn but clean sheets and military blankets. Apart from this there was a washstand which was supplied with a jug of hot water twice a day. Father Andrei then left me to myself.

During my visit to Poland I had been drinking almost continuously. My communist hosts took me to clubs and restaurants, even to night clubs. Now I found myself in an atmosphere of total silence. There was nobody near me. I sat down and considered what I should do. I decided that I would live exactly as all the rest of the inmates.

I lay down and started to read a book by the Christian philosopher Vladimir Solovjev which I had brought with me from Moscow.

After a while I heard a bell ring. I half opened the door and saw white-robed monks walking down the corridor. I was unshaven and was wearing a black leather jacket and black trousers. I left my cell and followed them. Nobody took any notice of me. A door opened and Father Andrei came out. I asked him if I could come along, and he answered me: "You are our guest".

Cross. Bronze. 1972. (0,48 x 0,34 m).

Fragment. From "Gigantomachia". Bronze. 1962–77. (0,82 x 0,71 m).

We entered a richly ornamented, golden colored baroque chapel. We have arrived, I thought. But no. We proceeded further and into a tiny, severely gothic chapel in the middle of which was an altar. Standing on it was a cross surrounded by barbed wire, as if it were in a concentration camp.

A monk read from the Bible. They followed a ritual. They crossed themselves. Knelt. Sang. I just stood there. I would not take part in a ritual the meaning of which I did not understand. I refused to act like a clown. I think the monks understood me.

Later I was always invited to participate in these services of prayer and meditation. It was not easy. They got up several times during the night. I found out later that those who could not take part because of illness or for other reasons, followed the same ritual in their cells.

Suddenly one day in the inner gothic chapel, I realised that the monks were singing a hymn with the title "Prayer", composed by my friend Bulat Okudzhava, a member of the Soviet communist party. It was at this very time that Okudzhava had written an article in the Literaturnaya Gazeta protesting against the fact that his songs were being sung in the West. A Polish communist had taken this article to the monastery and had asked me why my friend had written it. It can only mean that he is denying himself, was the communist's opinion. I did not know what to answer. But a Polish monk asked the communist: what is it you ask of Okudzhava? He is a communist, and it is expected of him that he conforms to the party line. This led me to realise that the Catholics had a better understanding of the communist party's collective discipline than Poland's communist revisionists.

One day I was invited to go and see a new church, big as a cathedral, in a new industrial area, Nova Huta.

Nova Huta had been planned as a modern urban complex, worthy of the new socialist Poland. There were excellent playgrounds, modern shopping centers and the best civic facilities in Poland. But the communists had decided that there was to be no church. Instead, a large barn served as a place of worship.

The inhabitants of the town, mostly workers, had different ideas. They wanted a church, and the priest from the barn took the lead. The workers went on strike. There was bloodshed. Finally the communists gave in.

I was introduced to the priest-cum-leader, a strongly built man. He asked me to write my name in the visitors book and I wrote there that their victory was also of significance for the intelligentsia of the Soviet Union. I was the first person from the Soviet to visit the church."

The Pope had given the church a stone from the grave of St. Peter. The priest asked Neizvestny if he could design a setting for it.

"I got an idea for it almost at once and made a sketch: A large male figure covered with chains formed a niche for the stone. The priest liked the idea and immediately found something else for me to do. A white wall leading to the church simply cried out for a relief. Had Neizvestny any ideas?

One came to me on the spot and I sketched a giant falling off a horse with a cross throwing its light over him. Saul in Damascus before he became Paul. Then I drew in a tiny figure with a large head, carrying a Bible; the transfiguration of Saul. The priest liked this idea too. I told him that I would let him have all the ideas that came to me spontaneously. He replied that he had yet another request, an idea for a monument to Maximilian Kolbe."

In Poland the memory of Maximilian Maria Kolbe a martyr from the war, lived on. This Franciscan monk was in the Auschwitz concentration camp in 1941 when one of the prisoners managed to escape. As a reprisal, the Germans decided to let every tenth prisoner starve to death. One of those who had been picked out, stuttered that he had a wife and small children. Kolbe offered his life in this man's place. The camp commandant agreed. Witnesses have testified that the morale of those who had been condemned to death, improved visibly as soon as Maximilian Kolbe joined them and shared with them his faith and spiritual strength.

Forty one years later, in October 1982, the agonised father who had survived,

Large crucifixion.
Bronze. 1974. 93 x 73 cm.
"Flottaren" Inn, Vansbro,
Sweden.

112

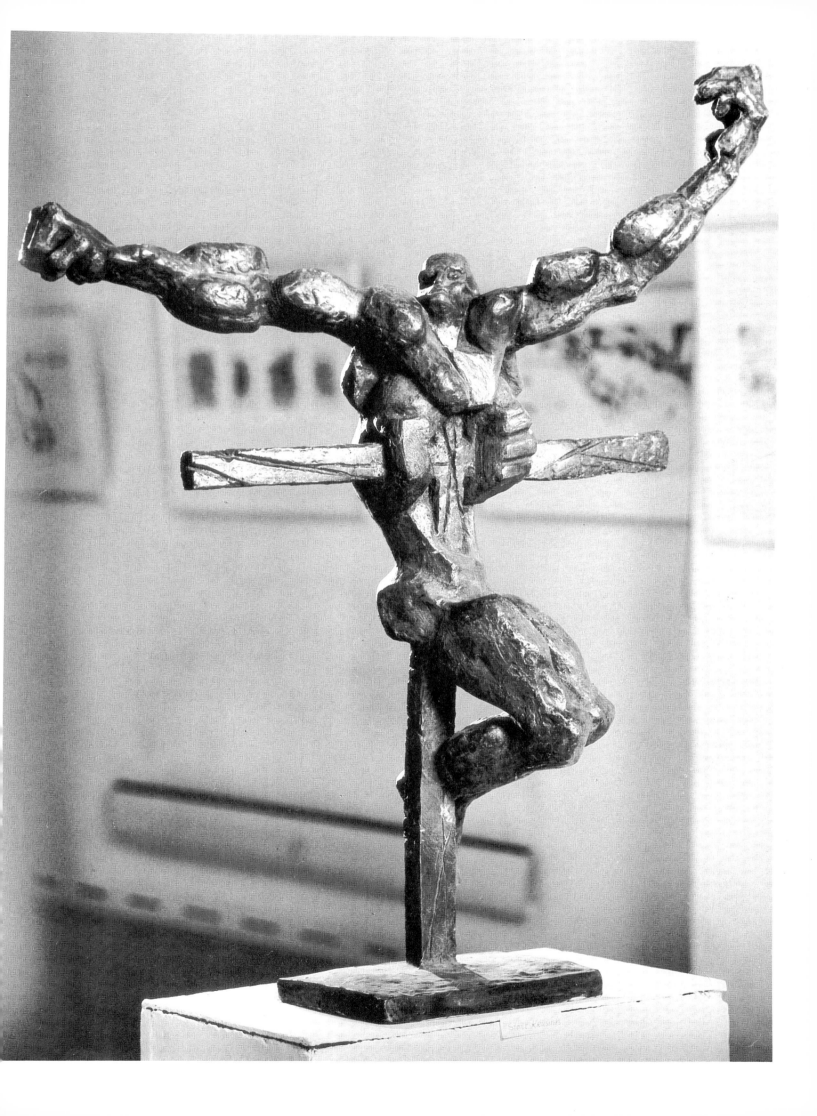

Crusifix with suffering mask. Bronze. 1974. (0,35 x 0,30 m). Art students in New York have asked Neizvestny: Why all these crucifixes? Are they not too religious and outdated as an artistic conception? The artist had to remind them that in the Soviet Union and of course in Poland, the crucifix is a revolutionary symbol.

Crucifix with dying centaur, crowned with the head of the Madonna. This work is seen as a symbol of Christendom rising up out of the ruins of Greco-Roman civilisation. Bronze. 1971–75. (0,59 x 0,45 m).

thanks to Kolbe, sat opposite Pope John Paul II as Maximilian Maria Kolbe was canonised at a ceremony attended by two hundred thousand people in the Square of St. Peter in Rome.

"My suggestion for a monument to the martyr was to have nine empty marble egg-shaped niches, representing the nine other condemned prisoners. The tenth and last niche would contain a protrait of the saint," recalls Neizvestny.

"These ideas came to me then and there as I was talking to the priest. I would not dare to lie about this. Those who were present are still alive.

Then the priest said: Here you see we need a twenty-five foot high cross. You must design a crucifix for us. As I had no ideas for such a cross I said I would think about it. We agreed that I should undertake the ornamentation of the whole church. He wanted to make an advance payment. He had no money, but he did have a good automobile which he could let me have."

But Neizvestny would not hear of payment in any form.

He returned to the monastery and worked on his sketches for the beautification of the church. Later, in Moscow, he made a model of the Polish crucifix which turned out to be one of the most evocative in his collection of cross motifs.

"I came to have a profound respect for my hosts," says Neizvestny of the Dominican monks of the St. Yacek monastery in Krakow.

"I believe in their devotion to God and in their faith in him. They live a simple life. Their intellectual qualifications could have secured them a comfortable existence on the other side of the monastery walls.

They were pleased with Soviet power in one respect. Whereas they once recruited their numbers from among the poor, the monasteries now attracted men of strong convictions and faith."

When Neizvestny, towards the end of his visit to Poland returned to Warsaw, he was afraid that his stay in the monastery might have embarrassed his communist hosts and friends. On the contrary, the Polish communists respected him all the more. And Neizvestny understood that the relationship between the Church and the members of the Polish communist party was far more complicated than he had been led to believe. The Soviet Embassy had however not liked his behaviour one little bit. As soon as he got back to Moscow, Neizvestny was cross-examined most energetically by agents from the KGB and the Central Committee. They assured him that the Dominican Order was the Pope's secret security organisation. They did not believe him when he denied that the Dominicans had tried to get him to work for them. Neither did they believe that the monks had refrained from discussing politics with him and had in fact confined themselves to questions of religion and philosophy.

The Central Committee forbade him to undertake the ornamentation of the Nova Huta church. In defiance of this order Neizvestny sent models of his designs to Poland, but as he did not get the opportunity of going there himself, he was never able to complete the work.

He did however find a use for the model of the crucifix. In 1981 when Pope John Paul was shot at and wounded in St. Peter's Square in Rome, Neizvestny remembered that the Pope was the same Cardinal Wojtyia who had his seat in Krakow at the time the artist had been so deeply affected by his visit to the St. Yacek monastery.

Profoundly moved by what had occurred in Rome, Neizvestny wanted the wounded Pope to have his Polish crucifix, but he did not want to create difficulties of any kind and was intent on avoiding all publicity. He asked the advice of Cardinal König in Vienna. After a while, the crucifix was despatched to the Pope through the agency of official Catholic circles in Washington. Neizvestny was sent a message from the Pope's secretary saying that his Holiness had received the crucifix with pleasure and gratitude.

The Day of Departure draws nigh

Following upon Neizvestny's visit to Poland, the authorities forbade him all further travel abroad. Some twenty or thirty invitations to the West had come streaming in. The municipality of Paris had invited him to an affair at the Musée de l'Art Moderne. Italian communists had sent him several invitations, as had the critic John Berger. But all was in vain after the Polish visit.

He was, however, allowed to carry on working in the Soviet Union. In 1974, Neizvestny's monument to Nikita Khrushchev with the inlaid bronze bust was raised. And in the years 1974 to 1975 he executed a monumental decorative façade, a relief in concrete, for the new Communist Party Central Committee building in the Turkman Soviet Socialist Republic. Against a background of geometric ornamentation, Asiatic profiles and masks are here built into a wall in a manner reminiscent of the style of ancient Mexican monumental art. This authoritative composition is held together by the eye and nose section of a centrally positioned stylised face. In its final massive format, the work is manifestly in the form of a cross.

A cross on the facade of a building belonging to the Communist Party! There was a furious outcry. Leonid Brezhnev, the Party Chairman, was to have opened the building in Ashkabad. He stayed away.

It was at this time that the witch-hunt against Alexander Solzhenitsyn was reaching its climax. One of the very first days of 1975 saw the expulsion of the writer from his native country.

One of the unofficial artist veterans, Oscar Rabin, remarked that now the authorities had got rid of Solzhenitsyn, they would concentrate on the opposition from the visual artists. He was right.

An increasing number of young artists had been developing both inside and outside the Soviet Artists Union, though mostly outside it. They earned their living as best they could and showed their production wherever they got the chance away from the Union's sphere of influence.

After the confrontation in 1962, the possibilities for doing this had been getting steadily smaller. Even at that time, Oscar Rabin had suggested holding collective exhibitions in the open air since this was something the authorities had not thought of when they had drafted their laws. In the meantime dissident artists were subjected to brutal acts of provocation from the police and from organised thugs.

In September of 1974, a number of nonconformist artists from Leningrad and Moscow held a joint exhibition in an open space on the outskirts of Moscow.

Neizvestny's enemy, Yagodkin, the ideologist, swore that this venture would be crushed with every means at his disposal.

His agents, disguised as "workers" made a brutal assault on the artists in the exhibition grounds. But the artists did not give in. Then came the notorious attack by bulldozers which crushed works of art and swept away both artists and public. The affair aroused strong reactions in the world press.

Water cannons were also used, and many artists arrested. The artists held their ground and sent the government an open letter demanding a public enquiry into this blatant injustice.

After a few days, charged with uncertainty and taken up with negotiations and representations from various pressure groups, the authorities under the watchful eye of the world's press, gave permission for the Second Autumn Open Air Art Exhibition to be held in a Moscow Park. Seventy painters showed their work. An endless procession of between ten and fifteen thousand people passed through the exhibition area in the course of the four hours of freedom that had been given the artists.

Thereafter the authorities tightened the controls once again and saw to it that all contact between the general public and free art in the Soviet Union was made impossible. Stubborn leaders of the artistic opposition saw that the situation had now become hopelessly sterile and left the country. About four hundred dissident and nonconformist artists were forced into exile in various ways.

Ernst Neizvestny's position was this: he was under constant artistic and ideological pressure at the same time as he had major assignments to work on. And more waited. But the authorities would not give him permission to travel abroad. In March of 1974 he called a meeting of Western journalists and announced that over the last ten years he had made fifty unsuccessful applications for permission to travel to the West in order to meet other artists and see their work. On this occasion he also made it known for the first time that for the past fifteen years he had been working on the "Tree of Life" project. He was well aware that by calling this press conference he had put his whole career at risk.

I visited Moscow at about this time. I tried in vain to get in touch with Neizvestny, but he was away. I was however able to study the conditions under which artists in a similar position to Neizvestny were forced to work. One of them, a gifted sculptor, had a studio full of cubistic, expressionistic works. These expressed what he felt as an artist, but had no chance of being accepted in the Soviet community. But since this particular artist did not try to bring them to the notice of the public in any way against the wishes of the authorities, he was allowed to continue as a member of the Artists Union. He was given ideologically harmless book illustrations to do which brought him in just enough to keep him from starving. The authorities were fully aware of his nonconformist production. My journalist colleague and interpreter pointed out the KGB automobile which was parked outside the studio. The artist, however, made no secret of the fact that he was being persecuted and talked freely about it to foreigners. He could also sell art objects small enough to go into a suitcase to foreign journalists and diplomats.

But as a creative artist he was effectively isolated from the world about him. He had been given plenty of first hand experience of what would happen if he tried to communicate with other people through his art.

118

Grotto mask. Bronze. 1965.
(0,22 x 0,22 m).

Ernst Neizvestny gave up. He applied for an emigrant visa. He admitted to his press contacts that he was unable to break the bonds with which he was fettered. He was incapable of making any headway as an artist and was therefore forced to emigrate for good in order to be able to continue his life's work.

He was refused an exit permit which was pro forma on Israel's quota because his mother was of Jewish extraction.

That summer he was the victim of an attack on his person while on a walk outside Moscow, a fate that had befallen other fractious artists before him. He escaped with no bones broken, but the warning was clear enough: the limits had been reached, and he would be wise to toe the official line from now on. Preparations were already being made to confiscate his studio and to take away all facilities for carrying on his work.

The Moscow intelligentsia, not to mention the international press corps, attentively watched the development of the conflict.

At last, in March of 1976, Neizvestny got his exit visa. This was in the year he was to reach the age of fifty.

"Two-headed giant with egg". Bronze. 1965. (0,34 x 0,25 m).

Torso of centaur. Bronze. 1961. (0,55 x 0,30 m).

Ernst Neizvestny had been married for a short time, a marriage from which he has a daughter who is now a painter. He makes very little of this episode in his life since he admits to being in no way a family man.

When the time came for him to break away, his former wife Dina, a deeply religious orthodox Christian, was in great doubt as to whether she ought not to try and dissuade him from leaving. Like Solzhenitsyn she felt that gifted Russians should remain in their country as long as possible in order to serve Russia. She went to her priest who said:

"I am only a simple priest. Ernst is both a bandit and a saint. He must follow his destiny. Let him go."

In the days before he left, Neizvestny's studio was a veritable Noah's Ark, where lion, lamb and serpent met. Party officials, dissidents of all kinds, journalists, friends and KGB agents in disguise. It was a farewell party on the grand scale. At the same time his sculptures were being brought into safe keeping in the homes of friends, among these the Khrushchev family's house in the country. The artist took with him quite a sizeable portion of his work, packed in seventeen large wooden cases. More was already in the hands of private owners abroad. However, numerous sketches and many finished sculptures in plaster and clay were destroyed by the KGB after his departure, so Neizvestny tells us.

During the last two years official monumental artists had visited his studio in Moscow and looked through his albums. Neizvestny was no longer making any secret of his plans for the "Tree of Life". With its wealth and variety of idea, he saw no hope of realising such a project in the Soviet Union. And in his mind he was already on the move out of the country.

The official artists reported that they had found an "academy of monumental style" in his albums. They closed their eyes to those aspects of their content that bore the marks of Neizvestny's character and metaphysical symbolism, and took with them

120

"Dying centaur". Bronze. 1967. (0,36 x 0,47 m). This motif is developed further in the centaur fragment of the Madonna crucifix from 1971–75.

"Centaur". bronze. 1967. (0,65 x 0,49 m).

the decorative elements of his style for their own use. According to Neizvestny they did not appreciate the significance of his fusion of opposites, but sought only to achieve a decorative effect by combining figurative, constructivist and futuristic stylistic features. A few of his old enemies among the sculptors who had scorned his art while he had been outlawed, emulated it as soon as he met with success. Neizvestny is sure he can demonstrate this. Something similar happened to Soviet graphic artists.

In this connection the question inevitably arises as to what kind of a state socialist realism had now got itself into, and what was now its significance to the Soviet community.

In an instructive interview with Neizvestny in 1980, reported in the magazine Partisan Review, Robert J. Seidman puts this very question, to which Neizvestny made the following avswer.

"I must say there is an excellent study by Siniavsky, *What is Soviet Realism?* But this study is an ironic dream of a Soviet functionary. Perhaps under Stalin, elements of such a Socialist Realism did exist. But in reality Socialist Realism does not exist; instead there is conformity. To be a Socialist Realist is to be like everybody else. Therefore, Socialist Realism can change but only in the direction of general stylistic features. Gradually, Socialist Realism begins to take in elements of Western forms as well, but as a rule not of personality but of general features, the worst and most banal features of various international salons because any kind of personalism is inimical. It is possible to take this thought to the point of absurdity when all Socialist Realists will become banal modernists. At that point an excellent realist will be labelled a bourgeois bastard, bastard in the sense of the illegitimate."

Robert Seidman: "This is a trifle flip, but it must be terribly boring for Socialist Realist artists."

Neizvestny: "Everybody is bored; those who put in the orders, those who execute

"Daphne". Bronze. 1963. (0,33 x 0,33 m).

"Mask with hand". Bronze. 1970–74. (0,22 x 0,43 m).

them, and those who have to look at them. Boredom is a form of patriotism."

Neizvestny has described the effect on him of these conditions in a book which he started to write after the Hungarian uprising. Through the years he has added to this testimony.

He outlines his views on mankind in the opening sentence of the book. According to Neizvestny, it goes like this: "There are three of us. You, me and everybody". They have three faces. The book deals with the inner struggle between the saintly "you" face and the demonic "everybody" mask.

Neizvestny has culled these ideas from the abstract conceptualizations of the famous Optina Pystin monastery. This monastery has been the spiritual fountainhead of the thinking of many of the great names in Russian culture, among them Dostoyevsky and Solovyev. The ideas correspond to his own spontaneous perception of the phenomenon that is Man.

He takes a pen and sketches a mask with serene features encircled by a halo. This is the face with which we feel the presence of God. It is our ikon face.

Then we have the face of the individual, the personality in the middle. This also has harmonious features. And on the other side is the grinning, horned devil mask. This latter represents Soviet power. It is the empty, collective mentality that the Devil stands for. It is the face of Stavrogin in *The Possessed*.

"My views on the collective mentality are not such that I am necessarily against all men," says Neizvestny. What I am against is that people should lose their personal identity, by becoming a member of a group. Then they lose their saintly face and put on a devil mask. This picture of mankind, sketched in the merest outline, is the key to my philosophy and to my art."

This then is what lies behind the very trenchant descriptions of the manifestations of power in the Soviet Union and of the various types of person to be found there that were taken from his book and published in the expatriate periodical *Continent*.

"Centaur) Bronze. 1973.
(0,20 x 0,16 m).

They are malicious word portraits executed with all Neizvestny's imaginative power and feeling for the corporeal and tangible. Or is it the naughty boy in him again letting them have it?

One day, he recounts in his book, he was standing outside the Central Committee building as the offices closed. A party member, a Central Committttee executive, and friend, had arranged to meet him there.

Neizvestny contemplates this unique sample of the nation's brainpower as it comes pouring out of the office cells and crystallises into individual persons.

I was literally struck by this crowd of de-indivualised masks, suits of clothes and movements. Gradually however, I began to be able to differentiate between them. I noticed that these people, released from their desks and flung out into the street from the upper floors by the elevators, divided themselves into two categories of one and the same race, not as individuals, but as groups. I labelled them for my own benefit as 'reds' and 'greens'."

The "reds" are usually the peasant type (the clodhopping peasant type, not the proud, aristocratic muzhik type). Expensive suits hang loosely on their frames, and they wear spectacles or carry lorgnettes. There is something about the way they wear their clothes that reminds one of fancy dress. They look well-fed in a curiously unnatural way. They are not just plump and fat, that's normal enough. No, these people have evidently eaten themselves fat on what for them is food to which they are little used. It seems as if they have betrayed their genetic type. It is obvious that they have been created to work in the open air, and that their forefathers were employed in physical labour. Their fleshy bodies, which have wallowed in foods over-rich in

123

"Dying person". Bronze. 1954. (0,17 x 0,20 m).

calories, have not balanced this with useful activity and have become bloated. Everything is over-dimensioned; cheeks, eyebrows, ears, stomach, thighs and backsides. They get into their automobiles as if their genital organs were in the way, without losing any of their caricatural pomposity.

And then we have the 'greens'. To begin with it is difficult to separate them from this homogenous mass of people. But when you look closer you will notice that some of these clones show a greater degree of imagination in their movements and general behaviour, and because of this it is clear that they are representatives of an intelligentsia that has in no way managed to attain the perfection of the 'reds'. You cannot hide the fact that you have a university training, and that you are numbered among the journalists, the philosophers or the historians, in short that you have a background which you, as a real person, cannot deny. Even if these people should be a litte 'red', the congruity is broken by eyes that are blood-shot with overwork and thus are very different from the clear eyes of the 'reds' which have not become dulled by dreaming. He who is 'red' is 'red' because he is so triumphantly red in color and is content with having been created to make unobjectionable decisions. He is one of that brand of guiltless Soviet personages who are capable of anything: from allowing a harvest to rot, to buying production machinery that nobody has any use for. They lose out everywhere, but cannot be ousted because they are never in the wrong. This total irresponsibility which lacks any historical parallel, is the foremost achievement of this social class. It is perfectly clear that its members would rather send this planet into infinity than stop this curious and sweet-tasting irresponsible behaviour. Unpunished they can spit on and besmirch the nationally most essential innovations and discoveries, as well as the works of art and literature that are the pride of the nation.

124

"Dying centaur". 1967. Bronze. 36 x 74 cm. This theme is further developed in the centaur part of the crucifix crowned with the head of the Madonna from 1971–75. (p. 114)

As soon as life demonstrates to these selfsame people that they have been wrong, and that the men and ideas they have persecuted have been right, well, they just immediately start to attend the anniversary celebrations and funerals of these martyrs of culture and art.

They give themselves the credit that belongs to the martyrs, and bestow orders and decorations on each other in recognition of the causes their victims died for.

They are content, and they are right to be so. They do no lie when they say: "Comrades, life is better, more enjoyable."

Where, when, in what age, have men possessing such qualities, ever had so much? Is it not stupidity, brutality, carelessness and wastefulness, in short their undisputed hideousness that is being rewarded?

History is no innocent virgin. It has produced many malefactors and sadists, but I do not believe that such incompetent victors have ever existed before. The task of the 'greens' is to translate the 'roaring' og the 'reds' into intelligible speech. They have to guess their wishes and formulate these so that the collective brain can recognise them as its own, just as if the 'reds' had done the work themselves.

A monstrous and thankless task, enough to make anyone lose his sleep, and which moreover ceases to be a creative function, according to the law of the organisational ant-hill.

I got an almost physical impression of how this dull, grey building sucks away their life-blood, how it gradually, day by day, deprives them of their initiative, their talent and first and foremost their integrity as human beings."

While we sit and talk of these conditions in Neizvestny's New York studio, he is reminded of the language of a Khrushchev, a Brezhnev, a Shelepin and of those about

125

them. They all spoke in a particularly brutish, primitive and unintelligent fashion. Theirs was the language of the lumpenproletariat.

In his younger days Neizvestny had a friend who was knowledgeable and interested in philosophical, religious and cultural questions. His mode of speech reflected this. They lost touch with each other, and Neizvestny's friend in the meantime won himself a position of power in the political hierarchy. When Neizvestny met him again, he spoke the same brutish language as all the others at the top. Neizvestny sees great significance in this phenomenon. Where they get their gangster language from, he has no idea. They did not copy Stalin, for he always expressed himself with clarity and with provocative simplicity.

"I have never been able to stand those intellectuals who create myths about these men, and who claim that they have so to speak been carried away not by dwarves but by giants.

I was angry and I said to myself: I am no Sartre. I want to look truth in the face. And when I had done that, I stopped acceding to their needs and desires. I no longer fell for the illusion. I refused to be carried away. I wanted neither a stick nor a carrot from these puny men. I had been forced to work for ten, fifteen years below the artistic level upon which I actually stood. I felt like the young actor whose one ambition was to play Hamlet but never got the part. When he had grown old an wanted to play King Lear, they came to him and said, now you can play Hamlet."

"Cross totem". Plaster of Paris. 1976–83. (0,24 m high).

In the West

In May of 1976 Ernst Neizvestny landed up in a small two-room apartment in Geneva, lent to him for a few months by Yul Brynner's sister. He had just been to Vienna to thank Prime Minister Bruno Kreisky for his help in getting him an exit visa by sending an appeal directly to Prime Minister Kosygin.

"I have isolated myself from the world and am living as if I were in a small village," he said. I do not want to make political capital out of my Soviet background. I wish to look around, collect my work together and establish myself as an artist."

While Neizvestny had been in the limelight as a nonconformist sculptor and militant in the Soviet Union, the curators of a number of leading museums in the West had established contact with him. All doors were seemingly open to him then. Several were to close again, at any rate for the time being.

He is full of hope and enthusiasm here in Geneva, and is planning fresh exhibitions. Standing on a stool on the balcony is a half-finished wax study, and on the floor lie gouache sketches of new sculptural works. In the tiny bedroom are several models that he is busy working on.

The seventeen packing cases from Moscow, big as concert grands are waiting in the Milan customs. The seven albums and the bronze "Tree of Life" model are close at hand here in Geneva.

He does not know where he will settle down for good. It must be wherever there are growth possibilities for his "Tree of Life".

He misses his good friends of both sexes in Moscow. He has left behind a position

"Centaur". Plaster of Paris.
Modelled in New York in
1976–82.
(1,5 x 2 m).

that had been built up at great personal cost, where commissions were lined up ready to be undertaken. He looks ahead however. He moves around his cramped quarters like a boxer in one of the lightweight classes, full of energy and resolve.

A searching question in this period of transition, forces him to cast a backward glance. Did he, either as an artist or as an individual, enter into a compromise arrangement with the communist authorities of his country?

"I regard the whole of my life as one great compromise. I never believed in the communist ideology. But at the same time I had nothing against decorating communist cities. I never liked technocrats, but still I accepted their help and the advantages they could get for me. But I never compromised on my art. There I did what I wanted.

I did however often make tactical compromises. I wanted to work, and I only revolted when I was prevented from doing so.

As an example, I was very nearly on the point of capitulating on the matter of the

"Large centaur". Plaster of Paris. 1977–83. New York (2,5 m high).

letter to Khrushchev. When that sort of thing happened, I would put on my dark suit, the one that my friends called my Central Committee get up. But then the naughty boy in me would dig in his heels.

It was said of me that I was a wily bird. I got mixed up in intrigues. And I compromised. But then I would suddenly change course. The naughty boy would revolt. That was when I was considered crafty.

All through my life I have been heavy on the bottle. I am not a family man. I have deceived women. But I have never been a coward. I could be afraid, very much so, not for my life, but at the prospect of not being able to complete the artistic work which I have in me. That is why I understand Shostakovich so well, and others of the Soviet intelligentsia too, who compromised on a far bigger scale than I did. I have an almost pathological physical courage. But I could lie sleepless at night out of fear that the authorities would confiscate my studio and not let me work. I would never go to

prison either, firstly because I could not work as a sculptor there, and secondly because in a prison there is no opportunity for female company."

Grief mask. Tombstone for a centaur. Photographed from four sides. Carrara marble, carved on site. 1978. (2,1 m high).

Here in Switzerland all these threats are now behind him. Neizvestny once again sees life as a gift; a powerful and intense feeling. In the months that follow, he holds a number of small exhibitions of sculpture and prints round about Europe. In the sixties and early seventies he was usually represented abroad with prints, and participated in collective exhibitions with a few smaller sculptures.

From the outset the market for his production in Europe was unexceptionable, and his work commanded substantial prices. Independently of his fame as a nonconformist Soviet celebrity, his work alone can guarantee him high artistic status.

But his "Tree of Life" project is not taken seriously. It is looked upon as a piece of gigantomania, and is smilingly ignored. Nor for a long time has anybody in Europe envisaged anything on a scale such as this. The last sculptor to do so in a democratic country was Gustav Vigeland. He lived on the outskirts of Europe, in Norway, a country which had only recently gained its independence. In the years between the wars, the capital Oslo used the profits from its municipal cinemas to finance an open air park that was to be filled with massive wrought-iron artifacts and a whole world of sculpture consisting of six hundred and fifty figures in stone and bronze placed along an axis over half a mile long. This is formed partly by a bridge with sixty statues on it in bronze, partly by a great fountain embellished with sculptures and reliefs. Granite bastions lead up to a stone plateau upon which are placed thirty over-sized groups of figures carved in granite and a sixty foot high granite column with one hundred and twenty-one human figures carved on it. It is called the Monolith since it was carved out of a single solid block of stone weighing two hundred and seventy tons.

What we have here is a gigantically conceived sequence of aspects of human life from childhood to death. This has been realised in a park on the outskirts of Oslo in a heavy figurative style by this Norwegian sculptor who was originally inspired by the

130

work of Rodin, and in his youth had done work on the gothic ornamentation of a Norwegian cathedral.

Ernst Neizvestny had read about the Vigeland Park in Moscow and had been fascinated by it. Some day, sooner or later, he intended to study it for himself.

One October day in 1980 he did see it. It was a great experience to follow the open-minded way in which he approached the complex. He recognised the monotonous and unexciting features of Vigeland's form language and the dull rigidity of his architectonic style. He was troubled by this. "It is after all by means of form that a sculptor expresses himself".

On the other hand, he felt that Vigeland had made a bold and independent attempt to put across his literary message without any fear of the banality or sentimentality to which the final result of his work often comes so close. He greatly respected the vast amount of labor that had gone into the project. Several individual reliefs in the small format showed, he thought, a genuine monumentality that was far more convincing than the larger works.

A vitalistic conception of life, devoid of metaphysics, pervaded the whole sculpture park. It could not therefore be regarded as the book of life, only as a chapter from it. As Neizvestny saw it, Vigeland's conception of the world was not in accord with his strictly academic form, whereas both content and form were in harmony in the so-called Life Frieze of Vigeland's compatriot, the painter Edvard Munch.

Neizvestny accepted Gustav Vigeland's need to break out of the salon and art gallery format in an attempt to give art the opportunity of fathoming the various stages and conflict situations of the human life cycle in one all-embracing work. In this he felt that they were akin. But he also understood that the European mentality was not ready to accept another project of this kind in the forseeable future.

Ernst Neizvestny turned his gaze to the United States of America.

Drawings and Prints

Ernst Neizvestny's prints have attracted attention in Europe. There are indeed those who find them at least as interesting as his sculpture. It is due time for us to examine this aspect of his work. The precursor of his prints as well as a precondition for them is the seemingly never-ending stream of his drawings.

His indian-ink drawings and dry-point engravings alone are an immense treasure trove. They represent the primary phase of the evolutionary stream of pictorial ideas from which a whole series of graphical works taken up with expansive, often mythological themes, book illustrations and paintings, ending up with sculptures, have been sifted out along the way.

Of all his series of prints and illustrations, Neizvestny himself rates the so called "Fate" portfolio highest, problably because it is closest to his sources of inspiration. It consists of 365 sheets. Every day for a whole year he worked intuitively to give graphic expression to the state of his subconscious mind. It became a pictorial diary to which he also added lines of verse. A running testimony of the artist's dreams and nightmares, his changing moods, his associations of ideas and intuitive feelings, all on the threshold of his conscious mind with its organising and censorious function.

Shaggy lines form limbs and parts of the body. Furious, terror stricken, totally foreign masks and facial fragments appear. Combinations of giants, female torsos and oozing organic shapes come into being. Flabby, strong, feeble, sensitive hands are hinted at in flashes. A mask weeps stone – one of the many configurations that appear time and time again in his portfolios, paintings and sculptures.

This is no pictorial world bathed in spiritual luminesence. It is closer to the *Inferno* than the *Paradiso*, to borrow from Dante, one of Neizvestny's favourite writers.

The spontaneous precision of these sheets bears witness to something mediumistic in his mental state at this stage of the evolution of his creative faculty. He dips into an underground stream. Only when he begins to draw does he see what he has caught hold of.

"I work then as if I am being driven. At the same time, I think, I analyse freely, I even theoreticise. And when all is said and done, who am I? A mad bull or an Apollonian philosopher? The dilemma is so deeply rooted in me that I am for ever searching for a way out. From this state of tension my formative powers draw their strength."

Usually the first that comes to the surface in the course of his intuitive creative process are contrasts, harmonies and conflicts. They are to be found in such symbols as the egg, the cross, the heart, and it is within the bounds of these that he seeks to contain forces that know no bounds.

At the same time there is a process of association going on. Mythological, literary, philosophical and religious themes are brought together with another set of symbols. Centaurs, hermaphrodites, dinosaurs, robots and crucifixes of various kinds. Political

From the "Inferno" series. Illustration of the XXVIII Song, verses 119–129. Etching.

132

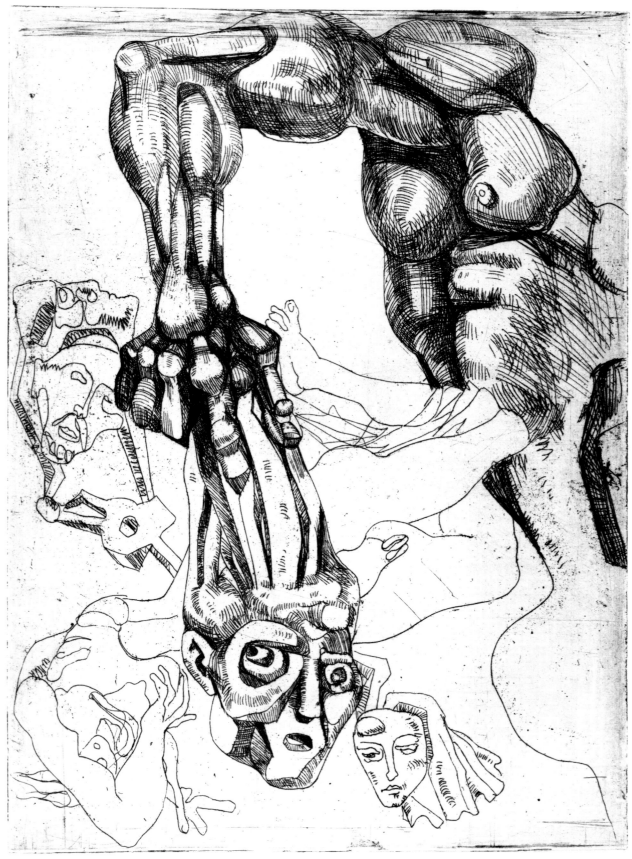

„Берцимиро"
g. d.

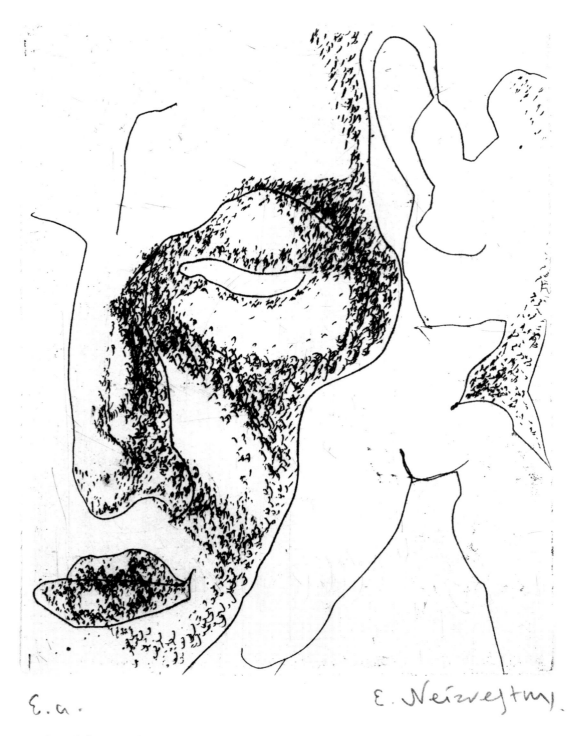

E. a.

E. Neizvestny.

"*Fate*" *series. Etching.*

and social metaphors are hardly ever in evidence, although such themes are perhaps capable of being construed from the form language that has developed in the supraliminal and subliminal recesses of Neizvestny's mind. But if that is so, it is as when a Soviet critic emphasised that Dostoyevsky's writing describes the miserable conditions prevailing in Tsarist Russia. That is of course true. But there is at the same time considerably more to him than that, comments Neizvestny.

"Such an interpretation is too narrow for me, because for one thing I sometimes do not even know who I am myself."

It is, however, quite natural for us to be led to think of rivers and springs when faced with Neizvestny's production of drawings and prints and sense the fervor with which they have been created.

134

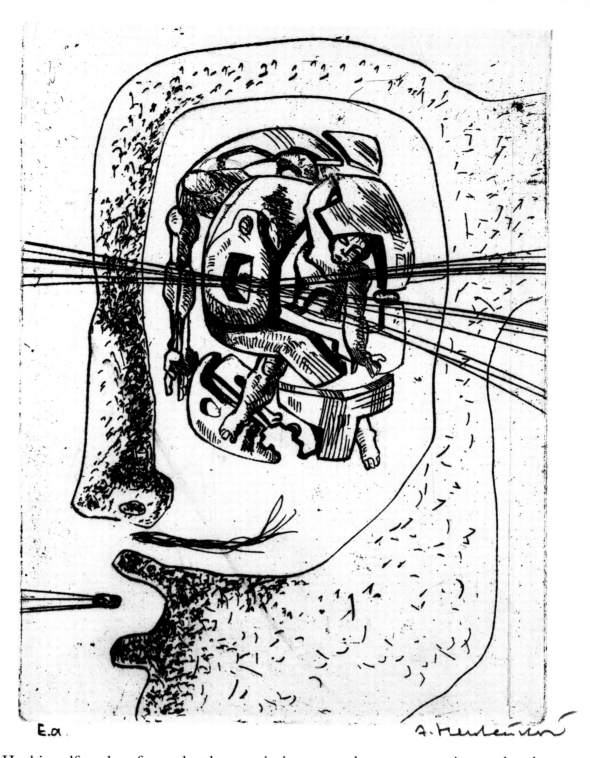

E.a.

"Fate" series. Etching.

He himself rushes from sketch to painting to sculpture, appearing to be the personification of those artists who have become so conspicuous as to merit the label modern. It would seem to be more important for these to be in the mainstream of a creative movement than to pause and work on the completion of one single artifact. Works hastily produced, the children of those who create on the move as it were, follow in their wake. Artistic values, time, motion and objectives all appear in differing interpretations.

Neizvestny has formed a theory about the "masterpiece" and the "mainstream". There are, he maintains, artists that first and foremost set their sights on the creation of the masterpiece, the complete and perfect work of art. In this connection he cites Maillol in sculpture and Flaubert in literature as examples. And there are "stream

135

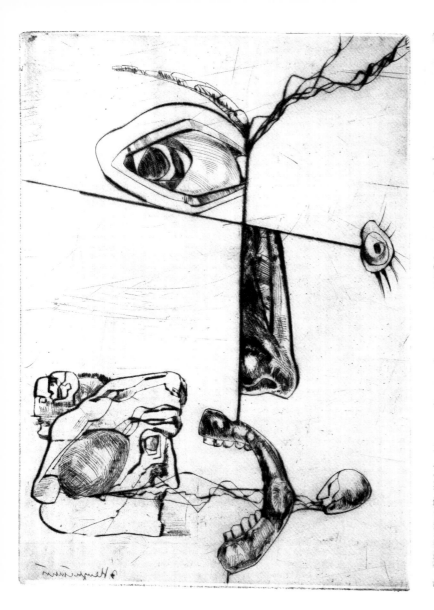

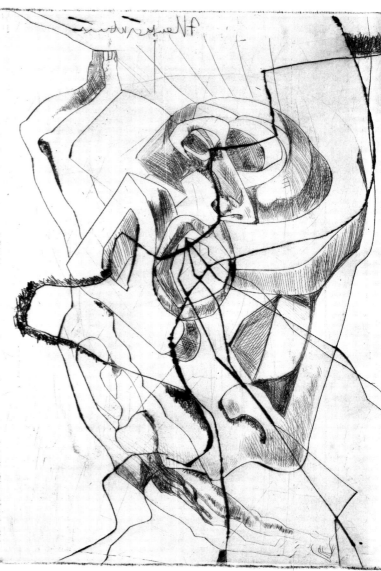

Etchings from the "Shriek" series.

artists" who are not at all concerned with masterpieces but instead are taken up with producing a steady stream of art. This stream is for them a matter of life and death. Picasso, Michelangelo, Dostoyevsky, Dickens all belong in this category of artist, despite their dissimilarities in other respects.

He takes his theory to its logical conclusion when in connection with sculpture he says, "I think sculpture represents not man, not an animal, not even a figure of some sort. It is not an object in space, but a continuation of the movement, of the progression of the soul."

In this category of artist, the most forceful have a dread of the turbulence of the current in the stream within them. They have need of some structure with which to canalise it. For this reason Dante conceived a plan for his Divine Comedy. Had he not done so, the forces of the current in him would have destroyed everything. It is all rather like the schizophrenic who devotes himself to logic in order to prevent himself from going to pieces. Michelangelo hid away in the Sistine Chapel so that he would not founder.

I do not compare myself with these men. But the way I feel about life is similar to theirs".

Perhaps this principle of his, like most others, is one that has been long recognised.

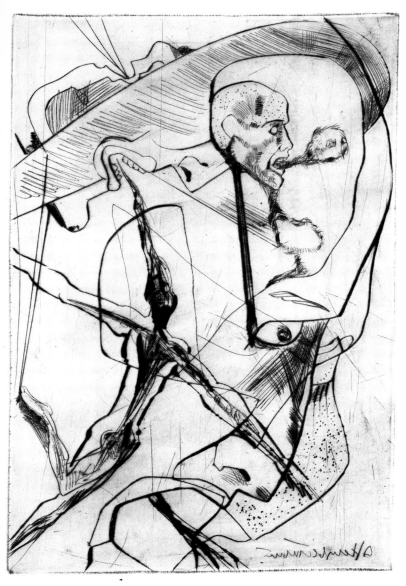

In Zurich, where Neizvestny still has a studio, he once assisted in staging a dramatisation of Dostoyevsky's *Poor People* acting as artistic adviser and stage designer. The play was performed at the Schauspielhaus in Zurich during the 1980–81 winter season. In the play the main character touches upon the foregoing sentiment in some of his misanthropic lines. He makes the common enough observation on humanity that this easily moved species is like a chess player more enamoured of the struggle to attain the objective than of the objective itself. "Maybe the whole objective of Man's ambitions in this life, lies in the continual struggle that is life, whilst the real objective cannot really be anything other than that twice two must be made to equal four".

We must now go back to the beginning, to Neizvestny's drawings. Originally these were a substitute for sculpture which is expensive according to Neizvestny.

"A host of ideas came to me. That was why I started to do rapid sketches on paper. Combinations of shapes occurred to me. Plato, Empedocles, Dostoyevsky, entered my thoughts, because I happened to be reading them at the time. This led me to do illustrations of Plato, Dante, Empedocles and Dostoyevsky. This was how the various series of drawings about them were born. They were not primarily literarily inspired. The literary aspects cropped up as the work on the drawings progressed and I thought

137

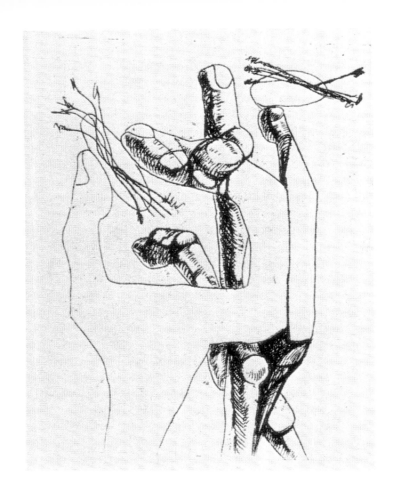

Etchings from the "Fate" series.

about the writers and philosophers with whom I was preoccupied. Gradually the series developed into graphic work of professional quality. But I never took these efforts of mine seriously. I put them away in a corner. But John Berger dug around in the pile during his visit with me in Moscow. He found more of interest there than I had taken out to show him," Neizvestny recalls. "It was then that I decided to buy a stock of metal plates large enough to keep my graphic production going for the rest of my life. I had envied Picasso his freedom, and was convinced that an important element of the facility with which he wielded his artistic talents was the fact that he was unrestricted in his choice of materials. If he needed potters clay, he had it close at hand. The same went for bronze and drawing materials. I read somewhere that he used the first money he earned to buy enough paint and brushes to last him the rest of his life. So I bought metal plates to last me my lifetime. When I left the Soviet Union I gave away ten crates of them to my colleagues.

I had made up my mind to transfer my attention from drawing to dry point and chemical etching. I would use the costly material as if it were paper, and just as freely".

But his graphic production became so extensive that Neizvestny had to stop working that way. Let us take for us one of his series of prints – the illustrations for the book about Raskolnikov, Crime and Punishment – and examine it for a while, taking note of some of Neizvestny's own comments on his work.

The illustrations were published in the Soviet Union in 1971 in a controversial

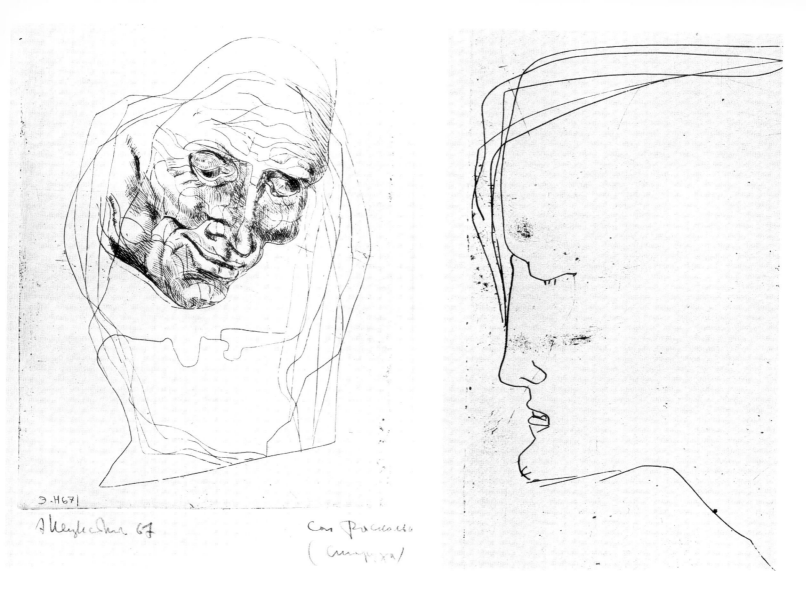

Etchings from "Crime and Punishment".

special edition of the novel brought out in commemoration of the 150th anniversary of Dostoyevsky's birth.

They are an expressionistic-poetical, pictorial accompaniment to Dostoyevsky's work about crime, punishment and atonement under the Cross, with Woman – madonna and harlot – as a redeemer. One clean, naked line traces her character. With the strictest simplicity of form, the same line sketches the murderer's profile outlining a tight-shut, suffering head, complicated, young, soulful.

A selection of twenty-four drypoint etchings make up this piece of illustrative art, the selection having been made from approximately six hundred Dostoyevsky drawings. Right from his childhood days in Sverdlovsk, Neizvestny's line had depicted fantasies from Dostoyevsky and Dante but he did not begin to work on them in earnest until the fifties with Dante and the sixties with Dostoyevsky.

Russian literary critics had maintained that Dostoyevsky wanted to write a novel of Dante's power. But I had the feeling that it was not really like that. With the help of experts on Dante and of Bachtin, the Dostoyevsky specialist, I got confirmation of my suspicion that the connection between the two writers goes much deeper.

Dostoyevsky was intimately familiar with Dante. He applied Dante's metaphorical and esoteric ideas and concepts to the happenings of everyday life. Like those in Dante, Dostoyevsky's characters suffer Hell through their bodies; in Dostoyevsky, that Hell is

Portrait mask of Dostoyevsky.

Illustrations for Dostoyevsky's novel "Crime and Punishment".

Man's own private purgatory. Dante's pre-Renaissance figures enjoy a fully corporeal existence, whilst Dostoyevsky's characters, according to Neizvestny, are nothing but heads that never stop talking.

He shows me a stylised portrait of Dostoyevsky in the form of a stone mask. «I would never draw a picture of Dostoyevsky as he appeared physically, since there would be no likeness. Tolstoy was like Tolstoy, but Dostoyevsky had so many faces that I came to the conclusion that I would have to draw a symbol, a sign that was representative of him. It is strange how this came to be understood as it was when it was used on the occasion of the 150th Anniversary of Dostoyevsky Congress in Geneva."

The face of Raskolnikov's inner-man, after he has committed the crime, is depicted as the face of a madman, distorted and screaming with an assortment of lines criss-crossing the whole picture. The effect is shattering. From where in Neizvestny's conscious mind does all this find its inspiration?

"Raskolnikov is the Russian for 'shattered'. What we see here is Raskolnikov's shattered face. I must add that before I began on these illustrations I had become

141

"Cyclops". Drawing. Indian ink and color. 1977.

"Hermaphrodite". Drawing. Indian ink and color.

Colored drawing from one of the "Tree of Life" albums.

Etching from the "Inferno" series.

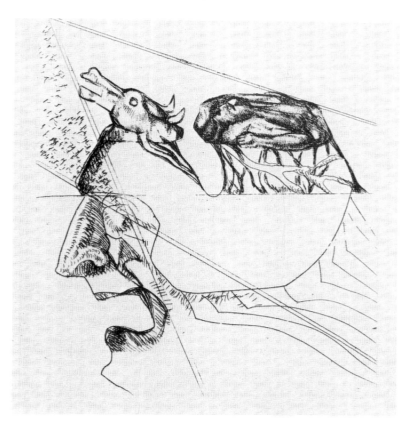

acquainted with the religious and semantic thinking that pervaded the Optima Pystin monastery which I have already talked about. Dostoyevsky visited this institution on several occasions and was familiar with its concepts. Many of the names he gave to his characters were founded on these.

Among these concepts we find that of the shattered face, which is not the same thing as a shattered soul. A shattered face does not involve absolute separation from God. But this is what results from a shattered soul which is how Svidrigailov's spiritual condition is described in the novel.

The shattered soul symbolises how the person in question is totally in Satan's power. But a person whose face is shattered can be healed and is not lost to God."

A friend of Neizvestny, a party official in a key position, had taken the initiative to have the anniversary edition published. He had on previous occasions succeeded in publishing selections from the Bible, Edgar Allan Poe and Dostoyevsky despite ideological barriers. He hurried through the production of the illustrated *Crime and Punishment* edition, making sure that each illustration was so positioned on the page that it tied up a maximum of type. Neizvestny's enemies were taken unawares though it was not long before certain elements in the Central Committee decided that the printing ought to be stopped and the book destroyed.

But the party official pulled strings. He found out that the person responsible for the decision was the chairman of the print Section of the Central Comittee, and spoke to him as one party member to another. He agreed that the book should be destroyed. But was he aware that considerable difficulties must be foreseen in that the authorities would not now have time to publish another book to commemorate the writer? However ideologically correct the decision to destroy the book, the fact was that to do so, would mean the loss of both face an money. Was it wise to take such a decision on one's own? Why not get the opinion of the intelligentsia?

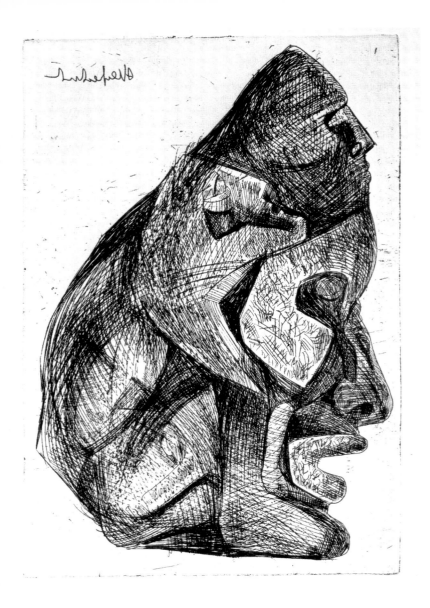

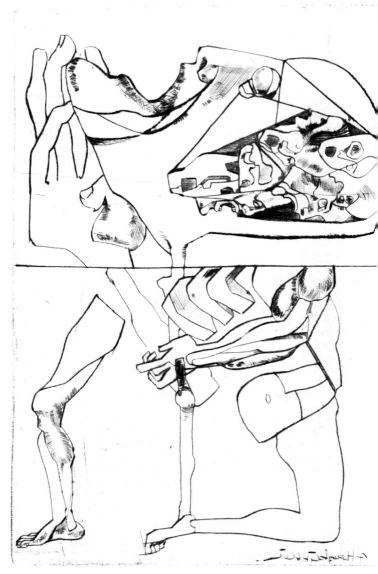

The zealous censor from the Central Committee started without delay to write to a number of intellectuals who he felt sure would oppose the book project. But the replies he received from the vast majority insisted that the book be published. The climax to the string-pulling was a telegram which Nicolai Konrad, a member of the Academy sent on the subject to the Government. He was Prime Minister Kosygin's special adviser on oriental affairs. Kosygin himself cleared the book for publication.

The reviews were the best possible from Neizvestny's point of view. Bachtin, the Dostoyevsky expert declared that the artistic value of the illustrations was comparable to that of the writing. Moreover they had "their own prophetic significance". In the event, the book was to a large extent withdrawn from the Russian home market and reserved for sale abroad.

One is tempted to conclude that Neizvestny reached the zenith of his graphic production with the Raskolnikov illustrations. Such an assertion is however rather risky since his graphic production is so very extensive. Among his portfolios is one on the subject of "Shriek", and one on births as they are described in mythology. He has made a series of sketches of hands, several Dante series, one gigantomachia series inspired by the statue of Pergamon, and many more, not to forget the "Fate", or "Providence" series on three hundred and sixty five sheets.

Portrait of Dante.
Etching. 1966.

Neizvestny wrote several pieces of verse for these latter. John Berger also wrote verse that was inspired by some of these sheets without knowing that Neizvestny had also done so. Lastly, the Russian lyricist Nikolai Nosikov wrote some poetry that was also linked to this diary of Neizvestny's. At the present time there are a hundred

146

E. A.

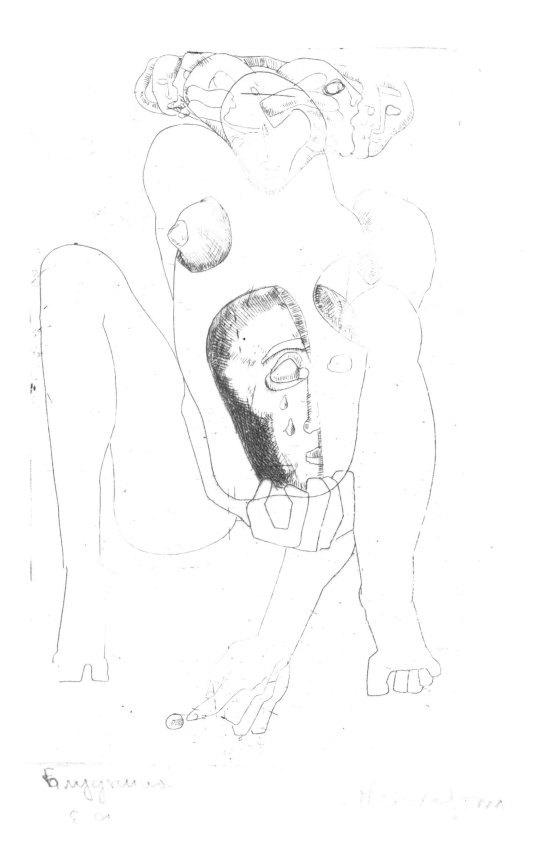

poems by Norikov, a hundred by Neizvestny himself and about seventy by Berger, all inspired by this one great work.

Neizvestny has prepared a hundred plates of poems by Nosikov ready for publication by a Russian publisher in New York. John Berger published some of his poems in

148

Illustration for Dante's "Vita Nova." The sleeping Dante's heart is fed to Beatrice by a demon.

the catalogue for Neizvestny's exhibition of graphic art in New York's Lincoln Center in 1975. These works were also shown in the Stedelijk Museum in Amsterdam. Paintings are also growing out of his discontinued graphic production. They are American blooms.

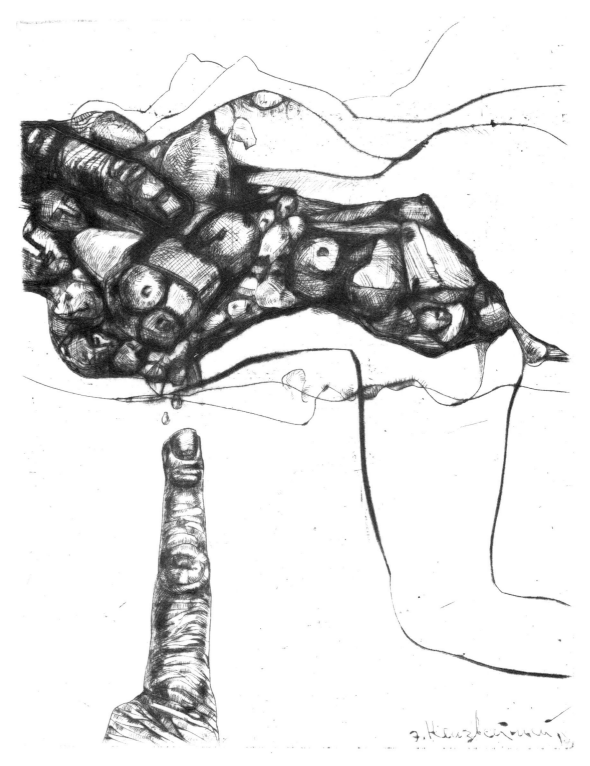

150

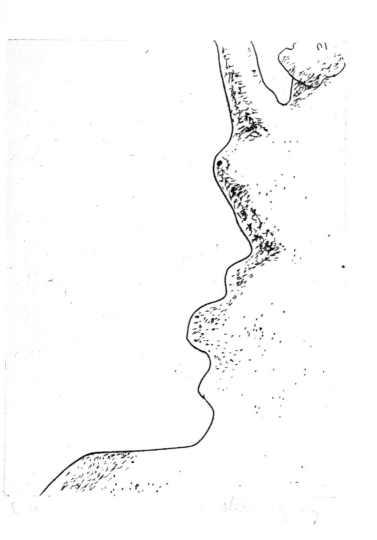

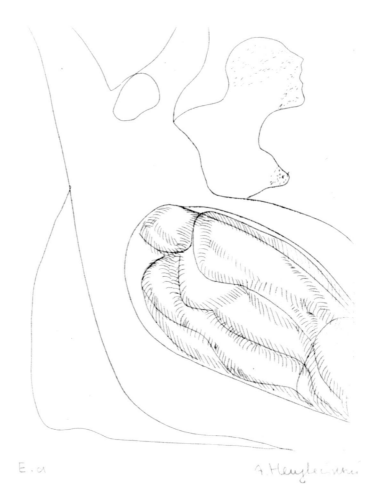

Etching from the "Fate"
series.

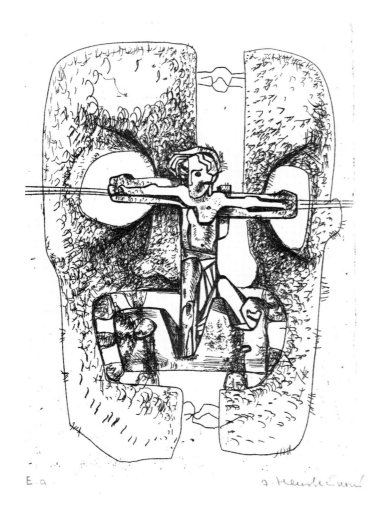

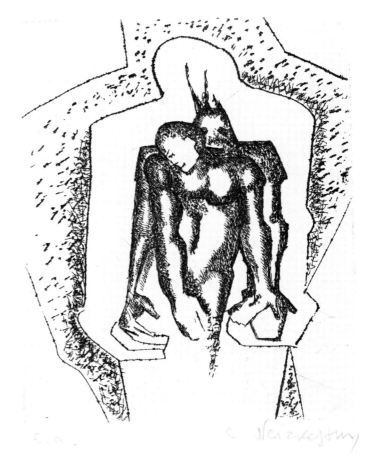

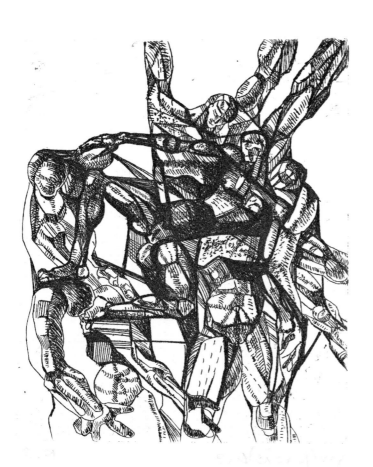

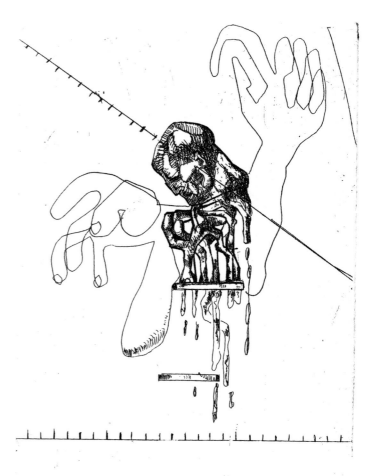

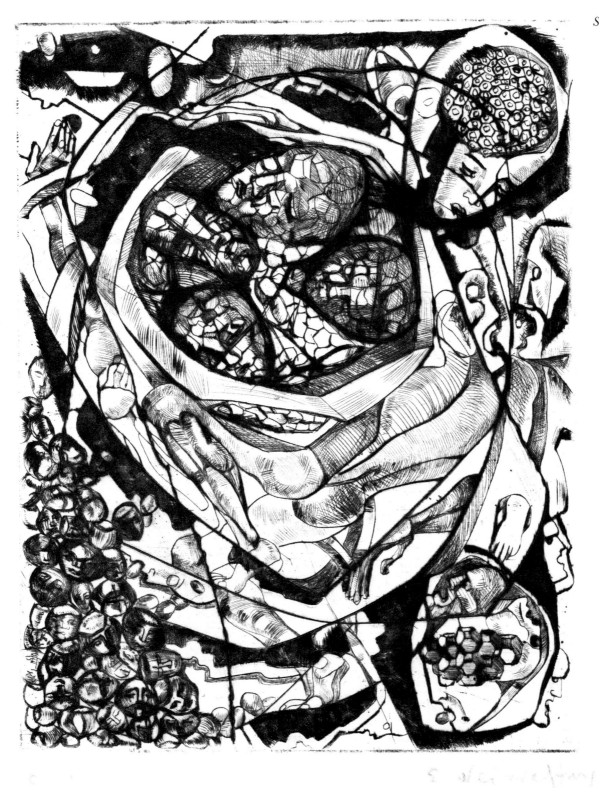

154

"Inferno". Etching.

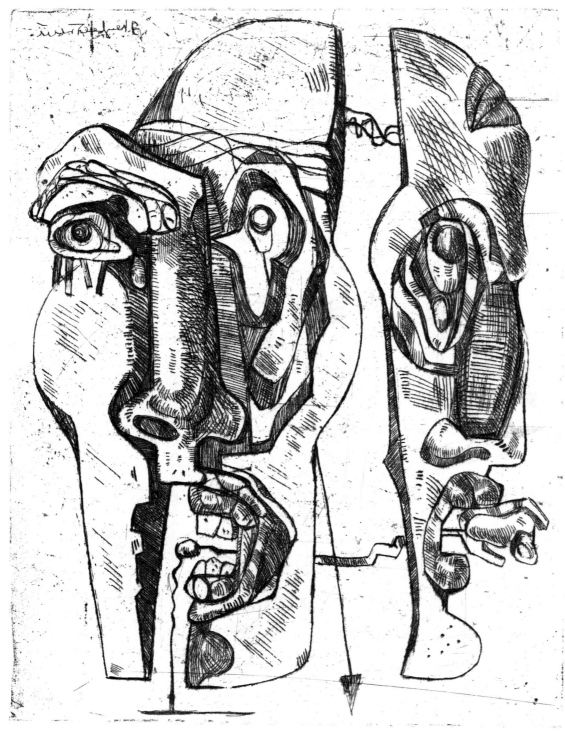

156

Introspection and Vision

Leaving Brooklyn early in the morning, Foka Rozenblat would arrive at the cold studio in Soho, give Ernst some Russian sausage for breakfast, and proceed to paint until after mid-day; just as phlegmatic as his employer was dynamic. Rozenblat had emigrated from the Ukraine on a Jewish visa five years back and had hardly bothered to learn a word of English. But he had great oratorical power with the brush. He had been the best poster artist in Kiev, a specialist in cinema advertisements.

Every morning one or more prints lay ready for him to enlarge and transfer by diazo reproduction to the large standard canvasses of which Ernst Neizvestny had purchased such an inordinate stock. Neizvestny had prepared himself for painting in exactly the same way as he had done when he took up graphic production. He wanted to be able to afford to fail to make mistakes. "Had I only had one canvas I would have been forced to succeed, and lost my freedom in the process," he once said.

After Rozenblat had pencilled in the outlines of the subject, Neizvestny would look them over, maybe reinforcing them here and there. Then the master would decide which acrylic colours were to be used on the various sections of the canvas. Rozenblat then proceeded to smear them finely and evenly over the surface. Neizvestny then took over, enhanced a contrast or harmonised several sections, and then put the canvas away. Rubens and his team of assistants could not possibly have got the work done quicker than Ernst and Foka.

In actual fact it was not quite so straightforward, for Neizvestny usually fetched the canvasses out again and did more work on them before he signed them. Every wall, even the ceiling, was covered with them. Their grotesque subjects – demonic masks, robot physiognomies, dismembered limbs joined to abstract shapes and highlighted with bold colors from bright yellow to blood red, from orange to verdigris green – stopped visitors in their tracks as effectively as traffic cops.

Some of the paintings had also been transferred from the "Tree of Life" portfolios which in Moscow had been given gouache coloring. The straightforward and at the same time richly orchestrated spectral coloring had been changed to brash effects. Hard, glossy and literal. Raw, insistent rock music, the incessant beat of which blasted through from young neighbours on the floor above, permeated the coloring. It had come to join the gang of neon lights, advertising posters, motor car bodies, the funnies and down town traffic.

Neizvestny had not realised what had happened. New York had got into his blood. That satisfied him. Never afraid of vulgarity he was looking for modes of expression that packed a punch. The synthesis of Pop Art and surrealistically tinged expressionism suited him down to the ground. He had conquered Moscow. Now he was laying siege to New York. "To a sculptor, form is what is most important. But if I am happy in my mind, I enjoy working with colors," is the comment he makes on his paintings.

Neizvestny's plastic form has also undergone changes since he left Moscow. But of

this he is perfectly aware. Unlike a number of other Russian artists in exile, the changes in Neizvestny's form language have occurred gradually over a period of time and not as a result of any hiatus in his life. In fact this applies to the whole of his evolution as an artist.

All the larger sculptures that he turned out during an intensely productive period in New York, were, instead of being warmly hand fashioned and picturesque, now much sharper and more precise in form. Lines and angles that in his Moscow period had been rugous and irregular, now had a knife edge. Approximated volumes were now precisely determined. Surfaces were metallic, bright, smooth and shiny.

Neizvestny saw these changes as the fruit of improved technical and material resources. The foundry facilities in the United States were indeed sophisticated. This he was able to take advantage of. The result was new, clean and exciting manifesta-

Face. 1980. Acrylics and oil.

tions of form. He had realised these particular intentions with the semi-industrial architecturally-oriented monumental assignments in plaster and concrete which he had carried out in the Soviet Union, but never with hand-fashioned work on a small scale.

The studio was now filled with plaster sculptures, six to twelve feet in height, together with a couple in bronze and zinc. An eloquent example of this work was a centaur in the large format recently cast in gem-like glittering bronze in the Modern Art Foundry in Brooklyn and destined for the Sculpture Park outside the Schulman Building in White Plains. It stood out in the room with its precise lines and shining sprightliness of rounded shape seemingly related to the axes of the skyscrapers and the curves of the clover-leaf intersections. The dark defiance and plethoric passion found in the figures from Moscow have disappeared into the background. But

159

*"Crucified centaur". 1983.
Acrylics. Painted in Sweden.*

*"Dancer". 1983. Acrylics.
Sweden.*

160

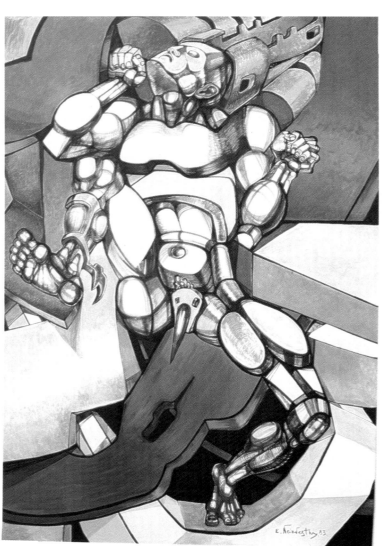

parallels were to be found in the Moscow portfolios of the "Tree of Life" in the way of machine men and combinations of organic and geometrically abstract shapes. Neizvestny a denizen of New York, was more than equal to the challenge of modern technology. But the primordial origins of the robot-like creatures were still giants, masks, centaurs, hermaphrodites and totem poles.

We have already touched upon the origins of the centaur motif. They are part life's ever-present contrasts and part self-portrait. The crucifix variants created by Neizvestny's hand are a related theme. In them we see the conflict between the straight line and the lively wayward line. Suffering and flesh meet metal and indifference. Expurgated peace is enveloped in blind passion. In the Polish crucifix which is part of the ornamentation of the church in Nova Huta which the Russian Communist Party refused to allow Neizvestny to carry out, Christ hangs as if he were enclosed in a mask and with a mask's inscrutable strangeness. But this configuration can also be seen as a female body with breasts which turn into cubistic "eyes", as soon as we look at the body as if it were a mask. The reverse side of the sculpture is in the shape of a richly veined heart – the heart of Jesus Christ.

"But my crucifixes are not merely Christian crosses," says Neizvestny. "A ship can be in the form of a cross, likewise a butterfly, a sword, the eyes and nose together, the human body with arms outstretched – there is a multiplicity of corresponding associations. The cross is one of the structural systems upon which sculpture is founded, like other basic forms such as the block and the egg.

But the hermaphrodite, this ambiguous figure from ancient times, does not belong in this category. Why is it that it is of such immediate interest to him?

"We live under the sign of the hermaphrodite, is how I see it. There have been similar periods before. They come about when matriarchies go over to being patriarchies. In the transitional periods, grotesque monsters appear and run wild in people's imagination. They signify a number of different concepts. This suits me as my work is concerned with uniting conceptions of this kind."

"But why the hermaphrodite in this day and age?"

"In our present-day civilised world men may no longer display primitive and typically masculine attributes, for example their physical strength or their prowess in battle or in the hunt.

These have been replaced by technological skills, which thus have also come to be manly symbols. But at the same time we find that women can also acquire the same skills. Women can put together a ship, or a plane, work with computers, push the buttons that can wipe out the world. A woman can be a journalist and she can be a prime minister. There are no longer any boundaries between the work and functions of men and women. There are even female boxers and weight lifters. It all combines to create an ambivalent situation. The man has no need to be so masculine, nor the woman so feminine.

But I do draw the line between the hermaphroditical and the bisexual. The latter is a biological phenomenon which has always existed. I am concerned with the philosophical, the psychological and the social aspects of the situation. Naturally the homosexual is more in evidence to-day. But that is not a cause, it is an effect. This is not the main point.

In the present situation I am concentrating on the female. The no longer so masculine man has become a part of the machine world, of the machinery of technology and bureaucracy. Women cannot be fully integrated into the machinery because she is reminded each month at the least of her link with Nature. More of our human and pantheistic origin are preserved in her."

"But you have now crossed over the border to the biological, which was exactly what these ideas of yours were not meant to be based on."

"Yes you are right. I have been talking about how I feel intuitively and spontaneously, and have not analysed realities."

162

"Do your feelings about woman not have their roots in the concept of woman as a concentrate of nature, as Mother Earth, and does this not throw light on a number of things such as your interest in primitive art?"

"That is correct. But in this connection I must emphasise that what is of greater importance to me are the masculine attributes of strength and virility. What I maintain however, is that technocratic man loses his deeply masculine Jungian archetype as well as his intuition. I do not say that woman possesses these, but in an

163

increasingly sterile civilisation there is more intuition and archetypical links to be found in women than in men. If we pass on to art we will see that women can produce excellent work, sometimes returning to the primeval archetypes.

But I do not mean to draw dividing lines between specifically feminine or masculine art as produced by members of the two sexes. In the final analysis, it is all a matter of art or non-art."

Against this background of Neizvestny's views it seems opportune to proceed to discuss his portrait busts which occupy a special position in his artistic production.

Here he swings between the naked face and the mask. The one extreme has found expression in a boy's head, modelled in 1954. This head delineated in clean soft contours, the guileless look, the attentive expression (large protruding ears) radiate a

occasion of the 70th anniversary of the composer's birth in 1977.

Neizvestny accepted the commission with great eagerness and would not hear talk of payment.

The day was to be marked with a concert of Shostakovich's works and Rostropovich was to perform the cello concerto which the composer had written specially for him. The presentation of the bust was to be made, not in connection with the concert, but separately at a simple ceremony.

But the Soviet embassy took action in advance and demanded that the bust should not be displayed at the center. The embassy officials disapproved of the fact that it was Neizvestny who had made the bust. According to Neizvestny himself the real reason was quite different. It was clear from the statement, issued by the cultural department of the Soviet embassy, that Shostakovich was regarded by them as a Russian state personage. Instead of the bust, they offered to present another gift on the occasion of the birthday concert, this time from the government of the Soviet Union.

Rostropovich and Neizvestny were obliged to give their answer through the medium of a press conference, which they held in Washington. Here, Rostropovich expressed his surprise at the way Russian officials had become involved in this very personal affair. He remarked with no little irony that he had seen busts of Beethoven in several stores in both Washington and New York, but that this did not mean that Bonn had intervened every time such a bust was put on display merely because Beethoven was German and therefore German property.

Neizvestny also decribed how Soviet officials regarded Shostakovich and his work, indeed even his memory, as being Soviet state property. And what was more, they considered that they retained the rights to Rostropovich's free will and the conduct of his affairs even after they had forced him into exile. This must also have applied to Neizvestny after he had been prevented from creating what he had dreamt of in his homeland.

This was not all. They even considered they had the right to decide what could and could not be displayed in the Kennedy Center.

As a result of the clumsy behaviour of the Soviet embassy, the presentation developed into a major media event with both press and public as enthusiastic participants instead of the quiet ceremony that Rostropovich had envisaged.

A sequel to this story occurred recently when Shostakovich's son, the conductor Maxim Shostakovich, who defected to Europe in 1981 together with his son, a concert pianist, was invited to conduct a concert in Washington. Visibly moved he stood before the bust of his father for a long time whereupon he spontaneously expressed his gratitude to the sculptor and his great admiration for his work.

Another famous Neizvestny portrait is of course his bust of Khrushchev in the

Novodevechy cemetery in Moscow. There are in fact several portrait busts of prominent personages, modelled by Neizvestny to be found there, including portraits of Neizvestny's friend and protagonist, the physicist Leo Landau, the writers Michael Svetlov and Galina Nokolaevna and the violinist Julian Sitkovetsky.

But the Khrushchev bust attracts attention for a number of understandable reasons. These became apparent immediately the Khrushchev family had made their request to the sculptor. As has already been mentioned, his friends Maximov and Zinoviev were of the opinion that the authorities would never permit him to carry out the commission. Others, such as Neizvestny's father, maintained that he should not undertake it at all. He saw the commission as a trap. Neizvestny's enemies would use it to misrepresent his position and to make him out to be an opportunist and a renegade. But it did not in fact work out that way at all.

After three years of intrigue and argument, Neizvestny was given permission to execute the commision, a decision that was arrived at after an appeal had been made to Prime Minister Kosygin from quarters that thought highly of Neizvestny's art. Kosygin, that stolid and conscientious administrator whose career ran through the period of Stalinism's alternating grace and disgrace, has apparently on occasion and unbeknown to most, played an important liberal role in cultural affairs.

The way Neizvestny tackled the Khrushchev assignment was entirely different from how he was to do the Shostakovich portrait. In Soviet monumental sculpture there were standard ways of executing this kind of official commission. Portraits of the "leader", the "general", the "worker", the "peasant" are all bound by conventional concepts.

But Neizvestny collected a whole mass of photographs of the deceased leader, cut them into small pieces and put them together again in a mosaic-like picture. This was how he modelled Khrushchev's features. From one angle one would glimpse a smiling, open Khrushchev, from another the grim party leader, from a third the energetic, go-ahead man of action.

Most people felt this to be something quite different from the official portrait genre. Khrushchev's old party comrade Anastas Mikoyan, disliked the work intensely. "Neizvestny is a really terrible person. I would never allow myself to be portrayed by him," he is supposed to have said.

While Neizvestny was at his unsteady zenith as a Soviet artist, he received a hint to be prepared to do a portrait of Leonid Brezhnev. Neizvestny prevaricated, and for this Brezhnev in all probability had cause to be grateful.

If we take a look at the whole range of Neizvestny's production, it is easy to become submerged in its imaginative scope. His flexible approach to the peculiar characteristics of many different subjects can often have a disconcerting effect. But in spite of its eclectic tendencies, this production of his has its own special character,

branded with its creator's personality.

Specifically, how did he proceed when, leaving figurative classicism (and the constructivist experiments of his student days) behind him, he found his way to the unitive, expressionistic, cubistic style that was to become his own?

"I can characterise the nature of my inmost feelings as being full of tension and stress. When I am engaged on some piece of work, I always feel that it is too weak, has too low a voltage, is not sufficiently high powered. Therefore I am always on the look-out for ways to make a work more powerful. When I employ constructivistic and cubo-futuristic elements, realistic or symbolistic fragmental shapes, and combine them all together, I am doing so on an ideological premise, although that's only one side of the story — I am also always basing my work on how I feel, on the state of my mind. I need these emotions to create the necessary tensions, the power that I need. Sometimes I can do with less.

It is never a question of combinations that are esthetically motivated. This is the reason why I intend to introduce light, movement, film, into the "Tree of Life". Not because I want to give expression to any literary symbolism or zeitgeist, but basically in order to reach the sources of power through synthesis. Synthesis is not just a theory. With its help I can express my inner feelings, my whole situation, much more adequately."

"Is there not sometimes a lack of harmony between the literary tendencies and the purely formal character of your work?"

"Yes, if I did not feel that the combination of the two made for increased tension, I would reject them. To me there is a direct connection between my ideas on synthesis and the state of my mind. My ideas on synthesis were born of the need for them. I did not just think them up, and then start to look around for thoughts and materials to fit them. Firm and soft, straight and curved, anatomic and mechanical, movement and immobility, beautiful and ugly, these are all elements that are more interesting when considered together than separately."

"Which is more like dualism than synthesis?"

"Synthesis can spring from dualism. There are different forms of synthesis. Combining things that are like, does not lead to synthesis. Synthesis is the joining together of different things, preferably several different things.

But the problem does not lie in things, in different styles, but in the plane on which they are combined. A man on a horse is not a synthesis if you look at the two of them as two different entities. But fusing them together creates a synthesis, in short a centaur. I am more interested in fusions than in the things themselves.

Everything is related to everything else. It is as in the Buddhist philosophy: the center is everywhere and nowhere. The more ties and relationships, the longer the chain of associations, the stronger the current."

"In your references to the 'Tree of Life' you have talked about a universal philosphy where everything has its proper place, rather like Dante's medieval conception of the world. On the other hand you describe the state of your inner mind as the spontaneous begetter of form. How do you reconcile the two?"

"There is no contradiction here. Since I must express myself in words, I shall have to use literary metaphors. The first part of your question has to do with how I have arrived at my literary and philosophical conceptions. These have evolved from my own need for tension. My literary and philosophical ideas have been shaped after, and not before I had identified the nature of my inner tensions. The ideas did not develop as a result of any kind of intellectual process, but came from a state of mind. This led me to Dante and to other related themes which confirmed what I had in me.

I want here to turn the spotlight on a mistake often made by contemporary critics. They separate spontaneous attitudes and inner feeling from essential intellectuality. The relationship is in fact more complicated than that. One cannot draw a line between culture and temperament. Dante's culture and universalistic mind are extensions of his temperament. From my point of view neither intellect, artistic temperament, nor technical ability exist on their own – everything is linked together, including the literary content of visual arts."

Back to the chronological order of the stages by which Neizvestny's sense of form developed. He discontinued his studies of other art forms, finding his own when he sought during the last years of the Stalinist regime, to give sculptural expression to his war-time experience, though not exhibiting them until after Stalin's death. Zadkine's expressionistic monument to war-torn Rotterdam has been cited as having been conceived on lines that were obviously parallel to these along which the young Neizvestny was also working as he formulated his attitude to his war-time memories.

He received at this time an impulse that made a lasting impression. It came from the big Mexican travelling exhibition which was held in Moscow in the early fifties. Neizvestny was struck by the feeling: "This is me."

"When I was in Egypt I also had the feeling that I had been there before; that I had once lived there."

"And in India a friend and I visited an old Hindu temple. There were a number of stone panels with reliefs on both sides. I saw one relief and knew immediately inside me how both the theme and the composition of the relief on the other side would be. The same happened with the other reliefs, none of which had been reproduced in books or other publications. Another friend of mine was a professor at the Sorbonne, with buddist mandala pictures as his speciality. He regarded my succesful guesswork as coming from my being a professional artist which meant that I had an intimate acquaintance with archetypal material.

He rejected all suggestions of supernatural or mystical powers. I am inclined to agree with him, but I do not entirely rule out that there may be some relevance in the theory of reincarnation.

As a student I copied Greek art from the so-called Golden Age. I was much taken with classical Greek sculpture, but I found it too monologistic. What interests me is the dialogistic, the state of tension between different elements and characters.

My youthful encounter with pre-Columbian art proved decisive. It was then that I clarified my attitude to ancient art.

I started to analyse Mexican art along with that of India, Africa and Egypt. I became more interested in their similarities than in how they differed.

I put a great deal of work into this. To take an example, I would place tracing paper over an Indian, a Mexican and an African mask. Studying their outlines from my viewpoint, I found that they were governed by the same laws. There were several such laws, but I was especially concerned with two of them: harmony and function, which I gradually applied to spatial structure and to form."

Neizvestny brings out a picture of an archaic sculptured head and one of a classic head and shows how the eye in both is so placed as to create harmony between the eye and the head as a whole. But a reproduction of another archaic work shows the eye as being greatly enlarged – formed in accordance with its functional importance.

"Eyes are the first thing we notice about a face. Children know that. They draw the functions: the eye that sees, the nose that breathes, the mouth that talks. The whole of the rest of the face obeys the functions; the whole body does so. Sometimes the rules of harmony and function work together. When we get down to basics, this is what taught me how I should make my sculptures: through combinations of the rules of harmony and of function. In poetry we find rhythm, disharmony and harmony, governed by the same laws as in music. The difference between a sculpture and a natural form, a naturalistic object, is that the former has a consistent rhythm.

Greek and Egyptic art have different rhythms. I find more poetry in the law of function than in the law of harmony. But how to transmute this poetry into structure, into form, that's the problem. As I feel it, Negro art, Mexican and Egyptian art are all superior to Greek classical art, since the emphasis is laid on the poetical as I have tried to define it. Let me once again take up the law of function. When a negro makes a man with a large head, a big nose, a small body, short legs and large genitals, Europeans think the figure is naive. But it's not a question of naivity, but of another set of laws, another set of signs and symbols, another way of looking at the world. But I was set on going beyond an art form based on function, on the eye that sees, the nose that breathes. I was searching for formal associations between functions. What is linked to what? This is a complex question. In some contexts eyes are linked to ears, ears to nose, mouth to eyes. There are innumerable variations. This is how my Empedocles series came into being. I was fascinated by his account of the Creation in which the organs and limbs of animals and man were originally assembled in an entirely different manner from that in which they eventually came to be. I also tried in a Genesis series to link everything together. This I did too in my 'Shriek' series. In Edvard Munch's painting 'Shriek', one can see, and almost hear, the shriek. But how is one to attempt to portray one's own shriek?

If I were to draw such a shriek, I would have to portray how I feel when I shriek, right down to my throat, ears and facial sensations.

The classical kiss is nothing but a symbol. There is no passion in it. But in Rodin's sculpture of the kiss, we take part in it as if we were looking through a key-hole, not pornographically, but as a poetic experience.

But how can one do a work of oneself kissing, of the act of kissing?

And what about the hand that I lay on a woman's knee? Functionally it is bigger than my other hand. Thus can function be tranformed into structure".

"As the principle of expressionism?"

"But here the inner form or rhythm often disappears. Archaic art, a Mexican mask for example, can be just as expressionistic as Kokoschka or a negro mask. But it is strictly structural since an objective rhythmic law is at work there.

I believe firmly and intensely that Egyptian and Aztec art are twilight arts in our civilisation, and not dawning arts. The description primitive does not fit them. We are primitive. The Greeks were primitive. The Egyptians and the Mexicans were not."

How does a monumentally oriented sculptor like Neizvestny perceive the monumental character of art? "What is sculpture?," he asks. "A work operating in space. The method employed by the Naturalists is wrong when it comes to free-standing

172

descends to grossness, to the oppressiveness of rhetorical monumentalism and its importunate hammering home of its message by dint of sheer size.

It is this latter that makes monumentality and humanity incompatible.

Egyptian art, in spite of its tendency to the colossal, its ritualistic solemnity, the massiviness of its form and its immutability, is exquisitely sensitive. I would almost call it feminine. Far from being a threat to its humanity, its power only serves to intensify it. Certainly, Egyptian art was influenced by the strict hieroglyphical system of writing. The ways the figures are arranged, as well as their attitudes, all have their meaning. But what makes them so phenomenal artistically, is that an astonishingly vital overall picture emerges from this rigid system, not in spite of it, but because of it. Lastly down through every epoch of ancient Egypt until the time of Ptolemy runs a hymn to Aten, to life and to the sun.

The act of creation is impossible without faith. How strong and complete must not the religio-philosophical convictions of these Egyptian artists have been, what a belief in immortality must they not have had, to be able to imbue me, a creature of the twentieth century, with that same feeling as that by which they themselves had been moved. I stretched out my hand in Luxor, touched the same sunkissed stone, and a quiet, but powerful "I am here" reached me through the mysteriousness of the hieroglyphics – that magical language of symbols."

"The Egyptians dimensioned their work on the basis of the block, which, large or small, will always be monumental."

"Correct. But what I was getting at about the formal aspect, also applies to a complicated structure. The number of elements in a sculpture is of no significance. The decisive factor is whether there is any clearly defined rhythmical relationship to be found between them. My sculptures for example, appear to be baroque, but they are not, because the baroque has lost this quality. But pre-Columbian sculpture has it. Lack of a well-defined rhythmical relationship between the elements of a sculpture, is the mark of the baroque style. The cathedral at Chartres was structured according to this precept. Bernini's sculptures were not. Bernini's sculptures have rhythm, certainly. He is a great sculptor, but his rhythm is linear, not structured. Its form sculpture in the round. All they do is enlarge an indoor sculpture mechanically, without attaining monumentality. Bigness has not just to do with size. Bigness is a way of thinking. A monumental shape involves the subjugation of space.

Think of the sphinx symbol. It can be made in a small format. But since it has the soul of a large format, the larger version continues to be symbolic.

It has solved the problem of linking the intimate with the grandly dimensioned. In the art of ancient Egypt, we find nobility and dignity all along the line from the colossi to the statuettes. Not a trace of cruelty, not even in battle and hunting scenes. It is an art pervaded with an unusual degree of monumental power, a power that never

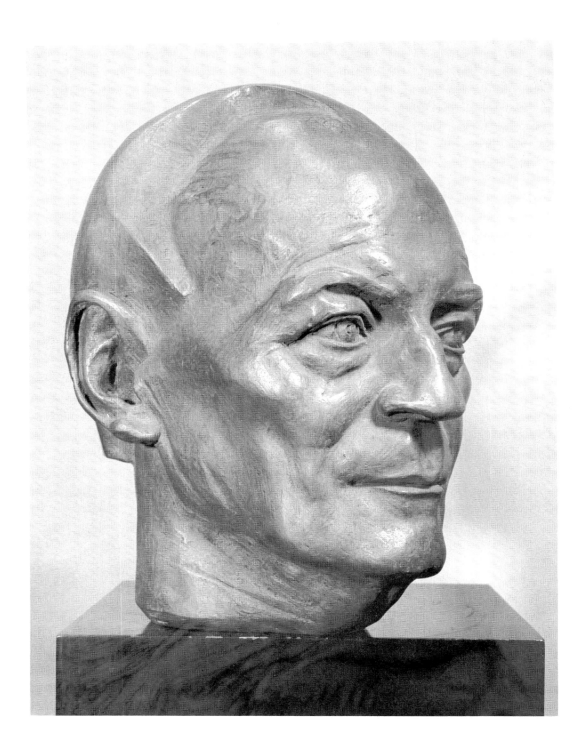

*Portrait of Paul Zacher.
1976. Collection Paul Zacher,
Schönenberg, Basel.*

comes from light and shade.

But a structured work not only takes in line, light and shade, but also uses them in a very precise ratio, which fits in with the sculptor's rhythm. A tree, a piece of coral, a crystal are all governed by mathematical laws. This is not the case with Bernini's sculpture which is a dramatic composite of contrasts.

I am of the opinion that Michelangelo was the last of the great sculptors, and that after him the art went into decline. He stands on the borderline. Those who followed, lost the legality which Nature could bestow and their work turned into mannerism and the Baroque.

174

I insist that my sculpture is not baroque, even though it may at a superficial glance seem to be so. An analysis of its form would show that its lines are structured according to the laws I have been talking about. The laws of the Baroque are different. They are found in Tiffany-art, Art Deco and Jugend."

"Now we had better agree on terminology before we go any further."

"I am against classification in art. I do not like the words renaissance, mannerism, romanticism, and not the word baroque either, since they all describe what is on the outside, and not the essentialities. When visual art ceases to be pantheistic or metaphysical in character, when it loses its organic structure and here I don't mean mathematical although I can imagine that the mathematical also has an organic structure – when all this is lost, art becomes something everyday. Where art reflects non-spiritualistic, anti-pantheistic human relationships, an Andy Warhol is, I feel, a super baroque artist."

To the Top or into Oblivion

When Ernst Neizvestny has had enough of the big city and the art business, he travels to Uttersberg in Sweden. In a closed-down railroad station from the turn of the century, two hours drive from Stockholm, Astley Nyhlen and his family run their gallery of modern art. In the attic is a bedroom and a studio which is always ready and waiting for the Russian migrant.

On the platform, now devoid of track, towers a block of Swedish marble, ten feet high. It becomes more and more of a Neizvestny sculpture each time he visits there. Its hard brittleness involves risks of quite another order as he hammers away at it, than those from fashioning the soft stone from which he so deftly creates monumental sculptures during his sojourns in Italy.

In Uttersberg he lays aside the cigarette pack and the bottle, and in their place a track suit is put out ready for jogging trips through the woods and fields, followed by dips in a river or mill pond. Sleep at night and plentiful meals prepared by kind, warm and placid Mrs. Ruth Nyhlén become part of the routine.

The work goes forward without sketches or models during the course of long bursts of energy on three separate visits to Uttersberg in Sweden, two hours by automobile from Stockholm. After which the artist can take a rest under the newborn centaur. The sculptor Klaus Ekelund helped with the rough work.

176

Fragment of a centaur.
Swedish marble. 1979–82.
Bought by the city
of Västerås, Sweden.

Ernst Neizvestny paints, models, reads, puts in calls to New York, Paris, Zurich and Moscow, and regains his strength. He has time to reflect, buried in this country-side of forests and manor-houses, not unlike that to be found outside Moscow.

"My situation in the United States to-day, reminds me of my youth," concludes Neizvestny. "I need elbow-room and commissions, preferably major ones. And to get such commissions I must have a breakthrough. I am only partly accepted in the American art market to-day. I sell my work, but I do not have a big public. In my younger years in Moscow free-thinking intellectuals and young artists showed an interest in my work. The obstacles came from the officially appointed, privileged artists. I am experiencing the same in the United States with the difference that the mafia of official artists and ideologists has been replaced by the official market, the Modernism establishment in New York. This is of course a far less intimidating enemy but no less of a monster; an anonymous authority. The comparison is also inexact in another respect. I am no longer unknown. I have completed a number of works. I have openings, I have made headway; I have many opportunities here. Though I lack the big commissions, I am convinced that they will come. On the other hand I am not so young any longer and time passes quickly. This last, though, has its positive side. What took me twenty years to achieve in the Soviet Union, namely an established position, has only taken two years in the United States. In this country too, there is a highly qualified circle of intellectuals who are interested in my work. And the young are with me."

Yes indeed. Young American artists and art students soon became so interested in Ernst Neizvestny that he found it worthwhile to start an art class for fifty or sixty of them in his Grand Street studio. But since this kind of activity could in no way be central to his work, he discontinued his teaching efforts. But he kept on a handful of students as assistants. Their experience of the Russian sculptor is here outlined by one of their number:

"He clarifies what is made complex through the interaction of forces. His works both mask and reveal life's drama. He uses the human body to show how powerful forces meet and how they react with each other."

These are the words of one of Neizvestny's disciples, a quiet man, but no tyro. He has studied art in New Mexico, in Europe and at the Art Students League in New York, and is now a sculptor, twenty eight years of age.

He is excited by Neizvestny's "maximal receptiveness to ideas and impulses, coupled with the authority and intensity of his creative work." His conception of form, has, according to this young American artist, in it elements of visionary art and strong belief.

"It stands on firm ground at a time when modern art often is out for effect and lacks depth. When you enter Neizvestny's studio, you are entering one man's whole life.

"The Prophet". Bronze. Schulman Building New York and The Sven-Olov Andersson Centre, Köping, Sweden. (1.55 m high. This is an important figure in Ernst Neizvestny's sculptural work. He envisages it as occupying a central position in the "Tree of Life". The Prophet's heart will be at the heart of the whole design. It will not be stationary and inside, it will be fitted with electronic equipment which will send heartbeatlike impulses to actuate all mobiles and lighting circuits round about the "Tree of Life". Ernst Neizvestny got the idea for this in Moscow and developed it further in New York in 1980.

When you leave, you see things as if for the first time, and countless metaphors occur to you. It is like a religious experience. He is a truly great sculptor."

What chances has he of making a decisive breakthrough in the United States on a broad front, and thereby also of being given the opportunity of doing his "Tree of Life"?

One of New York's experienced art dealers who has no difficulty in selling Neizvestny's work, gives a harsh account of the art scene in this world metropolis. He perceives some of the same tendencies that the young sculptor does, and is in

addition well-acquainted with the full compass of power politics and partisanship that exists there.

According to his evaluation, a superficial, effect-seeking modernism dominates the scene, supported by a small coterie of gallery owners, PR consultants and art critics. The major banks have long had service departments which give investment counselling on this kind of art. Universities have started courses in the economics of art, and international brokers have worked up a lively business in this field. They all service the newly-rich millionaires and the big corporations who are without any real artistic insight. In these influential circles art is regarded in the same light as diamonds, gold and securities, and treated in the same manner. Art objects often go straight into a bank vault waiting for their value to appreciate. The major investments areas are in American examples of the abstract expressionism and action painting by virtue of which the United States gained a leading position in the world of modern art, followed by Op Art and the famous names in Pop Art.

Imitations, variants, and a cult of ideas and materials following in the wake of these art forms, are flooding the art galleries and other leading fora of both the New World and to a certain extent the Old.

The art market boom of the last two or three years, with investments being made by people with absolutely no idea of art, was seen by this art dealer as sheer madness. "A complete re-evaluation of the human values in art is now needed in connection with a process of liberation from the existing power structure. It could happen soon. This country is always ready for something new," was the way he judged the situation on the New York art market in the Spring of 1981.

He took an extremely pessimistic view of the possibilities of getting the "Tree of Life" built, first and foremost because Ernst Neizvestny is not an American. "The United States likes to give the impression that the country is open to everyone, but this is true only within certain limits. There are wealthy people and corporations which would conceivably finance a project to put up an over three hundred foot high sculpture, but not if it were proposed by a Russian. A project of this kind would provoke criticism of the type – why has not that or that American artist been given the assignment?"

Our New York art expert is convinced that the project is especially unthinkable at a time when Americanism is back in the saddle under the Reagan administration.

But one of the influential critics that he had pointed to was not so sure. He has been watching Neizvestny with interest and has commented favorably on his exhibition in his columns. "The realisation of a project such as the 'Tree of Life' stands or falls on the generosity of one man, a millionaire on the grand scale, with sufficient enthusiasm to meet the challenge. There are such benefactors in the country today," he says.

The author during a visit to Ernst Neizvestny in his Soho studio in the Spring of 1980.

182

In this particular critic's view the easiest way for Neizvestny to achieve a definitive breakthrough, would be if one of the leading galleries were to take him under its wing.

Ernst Neizvestny has in fact been receiving financially tempting offers of contracts with a number of leading galleries for some time. But he has considered them to be much too binding. His production would no longer be his own. He would have to cut out art dealers with whom he already had an excellent, free relationship. Gifts would be a problem. His right to express himself freely in both East and West, even his freedom of movement, could become restricted. And most important of all, his commitment to the "Tree of Life" would foreseeably collide with the interest of a commercial gallery. He prefers to sell through galleries without any mutually binding agreement, and the galleries are willing enough. A New York gallery even offered him a comfortable apartment and a studio in a building which houses only well known artists. But Neizvestny preferred to continue to live and work on his own.

It was for this reason that he made up his mind to get away from his difficult landlord. He bought his own place further down Grand Street in Soho and converted it into a studio and living accomodation.

He is optimistic about his future in the United States, more optimistic than many Americans are about theirs.

"In the first place, what the Americans find difficult I regard as being fun, a holiday. I measure my life against prison, against war, and not by whether I have money or not. Secondly I have a feeling deep down that my art will come to be recognised and appreciated by Americans, and by them in particular. To-day they understand me better in Europe. But if you look at the 'Tree of Life' on its own, or at just a few of my paintings, you will find that they are more in harmony with the American character than with the European.

When it comes to the claim that I am not in fashion just now, I say to myself – why should I not create my own fashion? Why should I follow another, or others? Let them follow me. I believe it must happen. But when, is something I do not know. I'm quite sure that the breakthrough will come, at any rate after my death. But (smilingly), I would prefer it to come before then. Maybe I am pathologically self-confident. But that's how I feel it. And this feeling is confirmed by people's reactions. People are visibly moved when they visit my studio, not least young people. You saw it yourself when you lived here."

"The preconditions for the "Tree of Life" are space and psychological openness," continues Neizvestny. "Western European concepts of space are not as the Russian. A nation's philosophy and psychology are to a large extent governed by the spatial concepts of its people. Americans are more like the Russians here, and this is one of the reasons for my feeling of optimism in the United States.

I am also pleased that a committee to promote the 'Tree of Life' project, is being

184

"Centaur". Bronze. 1965–80. Schulman Building, New York.

formed, consisting of leading personalities from the religious, cultural and artistic life of Europe and the United States."

One of the objectives of this committee will be to help towards a better understanding of whatever Neizvestny may be able to contribute to American art and which it does not possess at the present time.

"I want to make something which does not yet exist", proclaims Neizvestny. But it is difficult. Everything I create is so far from what is considered normal in the United States that it either seems destructive or elevated. My work will either reach the top or sink into the abyss of oblivion."

*The artist with a
self portrait. 1983.
Gallery Astley, Sweden.*

Between East and West

Either consigned to oblivion or destined for the highest pinnacles. Art that is way beyond what is considered normal. Many will doubtless find Neizvestny's own appraisal of the position which he occupies, over-dramatised.

What is so drastically new and different about his sculpture and highly imaginative surrealistic drawings, etchings and paintings? Are there not in his work recognisable fragments of the long-since accepted styles and idioms of contemporary art; primitivism, cubism, pop art, deformed and adulating academicism and the like: in other words Picasso, Moore, Zadkine, the Aztecs, the Hellenists, Rodin all over again?

The real question is perhaps in which direction we should be looking in our search for something fresh and new in our time. The far-reaching changes which took place in the art of our civilisation happened sixty or seventy years ago. A minority of observers and critics were aware of what was happening and understood how much Modernism – this revolution in visual art – had in it of prophetic intuition, a changed

186

attitude to life and an acceptance of the realities of our age. These men were the pattern for later generations of critics; just as many of the pioneering artists have been for their successors right down to those who are working to-day. Many of them are still looking in the same direction, and their orientation will become increasingly rooted in the past.

A more worthwhile line to pursue, would perhaps be to focus on the more deepseated, more-or-less unformulated needs of our time, and on any potential changes in them.

This is of course a complex and quite impossibly diffuse assignment. But it is necessary to refer to it in order to be able to glimpse Neizvestny's present intentions. I hope that the reader will understand that I now at the end of this review, will be forced into an oversimplification in order to indicate the kind of cultural situation in which I see the impulses from Neizvestny manifesting themselves. Every word and phrase in what follows, relate to complicated phenomena, capable of being interpreted in a variety of ways.

The breakthrough of Modernism in art demonstrated among other things that traditional conceptions of the nature of the world, of society and of Mankind, of spiritualistic and moral values, had lost their worth. An impoverished religious and ethical tradition possessed neither the will nor the strength to incorporate the new scientific discoveries into its world scheme. It had by and large failed to provide the leadership which could legitimise the liberation of the masses and their confrontation with social injustice. It had ended in conventionalism, and in isolation from the real world.

Materialistic ways of regarding humanity and culture flooded in behind the wave of new technical and scientific understanding and the mechanisation of society and the work process which followed in its wake. Modern man rejected the traditional autocratic norms, in principle accepting that in their place, freedom for which there was a common responsibility, should be given an authoritative status. This was certainly necessary historically, and in retrospect would also seem to have the merit of consistency. But God was pronounced dead in the process. A dimension of unity in all this multiformity was lost and has not been recaptured, with consequences that many are still unwilling to accept. People today also appear to feel that the need to experience a sense of unity and totality in our being is as strong as the need for freedom. This can be seen forcing its way to the surface in numerous ways and with increasing strength the quicker the pace of change in our society, ideologies and human relationships.

It is in this context that we see Neizvestny's artistic initiative as containing a challenge both to the pluralism of the West and to the totalitarianism of the East.

The West became immune to the totalitarian aspects of Catholicism in the Renaissance and Reformation. The vaccine grew more potent both during the Age of

Enlightenment and after, into that of Liberalism and Industrialism. But the need for a universal view was too strong to be eradicated. It arose in the Romantic movement, and most recently led to a decline into spiritual imperialism under the two totalitarian ideologies of our time. The humanistic West mobilised all its resources against one of the two during the second World War, allying itself with the other. The West's great freedom experiment continued, while suffering increasing abuse and necessary curtailments of liberty in material matters. And a free-for-all conflict in the world of culture is reflected in the diffuse plurality of the art of our time.

In this context Ernst Neizvestny dares to come forward with a philosophy and a conception of art that is geared to metaphysical synthesis. He turns to, and draws upon, currents of ideas, views and opinions that have continually lost out in the evolutionary process which has led us to where we stand to-day, both in the East and in the West.

Admittedly, he also identifies himself with the world of science, its spirit and techniques. He sees the justification for it and its function, but for him Man remains the center of everything. «This tape recorder is only an extension of my voice. Television is only an extension of my hand and eye."

What kind of conception of humanity does he have?

The "Tree of Life" is dedicated to the Eternal Man. Man of the Bible, Dante's Man, and at the same time to today's Man, such as he has become as a result of the technical revolution. At the intersection of these two sources, the Eternal and the Modern Truth is created", he once said in an interview with Bella Ezersky entitled "Khrushchev was a minor politican at the time of Ernst Neizvestny".

He also confesses to the following:

"One thing is undeniable. I am a metaphysician in concept and outlook. Within the framwork of the existing religions I feel closest to the Judaeo-Christian. I honor the Bible and the New Testament, but I am convinced that the time has come for creating a new religion. According to my supposition, that should happen in the year 2000."

This pronouncement takes one back to the beginning of the present century, to 1912, when the young German painter Franz Marc and Neizvestny's compatriot Wassily Kandinsky published the almanac *Der blaue Reiter* in Germany.

On the subject of the artists of the modern breakthrough Marc wrote: "Their thinking has another goal (and not that concerned with the interpretation and further development of Impressionism): to create through their efforts contemporary symbols which will have their place on the altars of the future spiritual religion. (. . .) One feels in truth that this has to do with a new religion that as yet has no evangelist and has not so far won recognition anywhere."

Similar notions and opinions were to be found in Kandinsky's book *Über das Geistige in der Kunst,* which appeared the previous year. They had their origins in orthodox Christianity and a spiritual tradition existing on Russian as well as Germanic soil.

This "holy Russia" concept also flickers, as we have seen, through Ernst Neizvestny's Russian-Jewish pugilist physiognomy; "both a saint and a bandit", as his wife's priest saw him.

Russian Christianity's understanding of Man and the realities of life shines through the writings of a Dostoyevsky and a Solzhenitsyn. It was the mainstay of Dostoyevsky's belief that Russia had a great mission as a redeemer of Mankind, first and foremost in the rationalistic and divided West. From these sources Russian spiritualistic philosophers from Solovyov to Berdyaev, have drawn their inspiration.

But on the fall of the tsarist régime this typically Russian source of spiritual strength lost out in the struggle for the control of the future of the empire and of the people. It did not in fact seem to be in the picture at all during the decisive period in October 1917. Maybe the tragedy was first and foremost one that has repeated itself again and again in our history, when spiritualistic dedication has tended to orientate itself vertically on a merely spiritual plane, neglecting the scientific and socially pragmatic horizontal planes of the real world, to borrow Neizvestny's cross analogy. The latter dimension was one over which Lenin and his marxists had specially trained themselves to exercise control. However, before the Russian revolution consolidated itself, there seemed to exist a feverishly spiritualistic process of transformation directed towards the establishment of supremacies in fields outside power politics.

With unprecedented daring this manifested itself in the visual arts.

The two Russian leaders in the breakthrough for non-figurative art, Wassily Kandinsky and Kasimir Malevich saw this art both as a result of, and as an expression of, a spiritualistic conception of life and reality in a form satisfying the needs of the time. When we consider the "timeless" platonic structural composition which is prevalent in Russian ikon painting with its roots in Greek Byzantinism, we can glimpse the philosophical and formal foundations upon which is built the suprematism of, not least, Malevich.

The final period of the Tsarist régime saw the new artistic movements bubbling up in several places. With great enthusiasm they gained strength during the initial heroic-tragic period of the Revolution, seeing themselves as its forerunners and its masters of form.

And so it was that artists took on an unprecedented variety of functions in society, mainly on an experimental scale, and with the more or less tentative approval of the cultural leaders in the new political system.

First among these was Lunarcharsky, the commissar mentioned by Khrushchev in his account of his youth. Lenin was never in favor of these impulses, but he had his hands full with tasks of greater urgency in this new Soviet republic which was fighting for its life, torn by civil war, suffering from famine, and deficient in resources of all kinds.

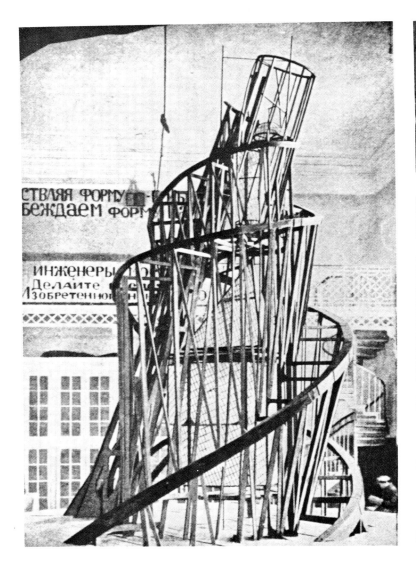

The avant-garde groups had differing objectives and fought each other bitterly. Ideologies and counter-ideologies sprang up with great rapidity, and in retrospect it is difficult to differentiate between them.

Here, some clarification can be found in Camilla Grey's book *The Russian Experiment in Art* (1863–1922), published in 1962.

Three groupings of these left-wing artists are of interest to our theme. One was dominated by Kandinsky, Malevich and the Pevsner brothers. They maintained that art was a spiritual process the object of which was the formulation of Man's view of the world. At the other extreme stood a materialistic constructivist ideology which aimed at "bringing Art into Life". The artist was to be an "artist-engineer" and build bridges between art and the mechanics of the new technological civilisation. The constructivists hoped to accelerate the process of liberating the people from the want and toil that had enslaved it all through history. Their form language was based on geometry.

The new Man would dominate the world by virtue of the new civilisation that he had built. But linked up with the image of the machine, this master of the universe would himself risk becoming a robot-like being.

190

Both the East and the West have in the process of time been exposed to the overwhelming material results of this philosophy of technological evolution. Its introduction into Neizvestny's art is a theme charged with negative associations. But when it comes to the constructivist views on the new mission of the artist as one who intervenes in the shaping of society with decisive effect, he is more in harmony with them.

He has quite a different relationship to the third set of impulses from this pioneer period. It had its effect on him, first and foremost through Vladimir Tatlin, who also had visions of Man's future in a technological age. He was never a member of the group of constructivists, though they themselves were stimulated by this strange innovator who preferred to work on his own in a small studio with only a few assistants. But the fundamental idea upon which his art is based, must have been hard for them to stomach.

In contrast to the constructivists, Tatlin based his form language on organic structures. The laws of Nature would be the foundation upon which the new techically oriented culture was to be built. Tatlin studied winged insects in order to design an aeroplane according to Nature's principles, experiments which it is said have been reinstituted in to-day's Soviet Union.

Goethe felt the products of his creative genius grow within him with the same force of necessity as that which causes a plant to flower. "The artist realises Nature's ideas", is a concept that was also shared by the non-figurative Kandinsky. It was apparent that it was this concept, based on the inner laws of Man and Nature, that Tatlin tried to expand in order to create a new industrial technology.

If we follow up Neizvestny's assertion that such Russian modernists as Malevich and Tatlin cannot be understood without reference to the earlier figure of Nikolai F. Feyodorov (1828–1903) we find that their otherwise differently oriented technological ideology is given yet further spiritualistic support.

But it is difficult to establish this with any degree of certainty since we have to do with an unusually diffident person. Feyodorov's most important writings were printed by his students privately in five hundred copies after his death, and given away to those who had need of them. This man could very well be one of the hidden key figures in the history of Russian culture. Dostoyevsky said of his ideas: «Fundamentally I agree with these thoughts; I read them as my own." Solovyov read the manuscript of Feyodorov's plan of the world at one sitting and formulated his reaction in a letter to the author thus:

"I will only say that since the appearance of Christianity, your plan is the first forward movement of the human spirit along the way of Christ. For my part, I can but acknowledge you as my leader and spiritual father."

And Tolstoy who knew the austere Moscow librarian well, observed to Fet, the poet: "I am proud to live in the same century as such a man. "To his son, Tolstoy said: "If saints exist, they must be like him."

Here are some observations by Feyodorov which have relevance to our theme:

"Nature as she exists today – due to mankind's ignorance and immorality – cannot be considered God's creation, for in her His intentions are partly unfulfilled and partly distorted . . ."

"Our relationship with Nature should be supplanted by a conscious, powerful regulation of Nature, by an all-embracing, perfect will of humanity towards a lofty moral goal . . ."

"The aim of all human efforts is to secure for everyone a healthy, moral, happy existence, including victory over hunger, over disasters caused by the elements, illness, imperfections in the human organism, and finally over death itself."

The final perspective in Feyodorov's thinking included our forefathers. He seems to have meant that it comes within the bounds of possibility for men to waken the dead; indeed that it was their duty to do so. These were thoughts with which neither Dostoyevsky nor Solovyov wished to be associated, and it furnishes us with a reasonable explanation of Feyodorov's eclipse.

But his view of Mankind as the creative instrument of God, destined to better the world by means of a thoroughgoing and morally fine-tuned exploitation of the possibilities of the techno-scientific civilisation, did in the event stimulate the constructivist prophets and utopians of Tatlin's genre.

Vladimir Tatlin's creative activity culminated in a project to erect a dynamic tower structure in Moscow's Red Square, twice the height of the Empire State Building. The Soviet Ministry of Culture commisioned the tower as a monument to the Third International, and Tatlin and his assistants worked on it for more than two years. The original design, was, according to Tatlin, envisaged as "a union of purely artistic forms, (painting, sculpture and architecture) for a utilitarian purpose."

It was to be a rotating construction and the public were to be transported in all directions by mechanical means. A framework in the form of a spiral would support a long glass-clad body made up of a cylinder, a cone and a glass cube. This was to reach out along an asymmetric axis like a leaning Eiffel Tower, a continuation out into space of the spiral flow. Lectures, congresses and conferences would be held in the lower cylindrical section which would take a whole year to rotate fully, The cone, which would take a month to rotate, was to house administrative and management functions. The upper cube-shaped glass structure would rotate fully once a day and house an information center, issuing bulletins and manifestos continuously by means of the telegraph, the telephone, radio, loudspeakers and, when darkness fell, on an enormous film screen. On dark, heavily clouded evenings, messages and slogans would be projected into the sky.

Large crucifixion. Acrylics and oil. 1982. (2 x 2,4 m).

Is there not a striking similarity between Tatlin's Third International spiral tower and Neizvestny's "Tree of Life"?

Both are a synthesis of architecture and sculpture, envisaged on the grand scale; dynamic spiral mobiles housing a great variety of everyday activities. With their many different functions fused into one highly unconventional whole, the two monuments are related. Both are the fruits of conscious efforts to cross frontiers, and form an all-embracing view of our age in artistic terms.

May one not, even if it is questionable to juggle with what is national in a nation's culture, be allowed to suggest that we are here faced with something typically Russian? What other people in our part of the world has up to this day so characteristically preserved both the need and the ability to see the universe as an entirety, which naturally also includes the marxist experiment?

From our point of view, the dissimilarities between Tatlin's and Neizvestny's projects are more interesting than their similarities. The "Tree of Life" is more subtle in style and far richer in form and content. Its conception is more manifold, far more open, and above all linked to a spiritual dimension such as has manifested itself throughout the history of mankind. For Tatlin's conception there could be found a place in the "Tree of Life", but there is no place for Neizvestny's in the Third International's Red Square tower.

But it is wise to have a care. Where in point of fact is that Christian spiritualism that Neizvestny so often talks about, to be found in his production? The occasions when

193

"Mental Cry II."
Mixed media.
195 x 150 cm

the "ikon face" with timeless unselfish love illuminates this torrent of passion, fantasy and conflict, are indeed few and far between.

Ernst Neizvestny uses the crucifix motif frequently in a variety of contexts. He follows the whole sequence of events on Calvary down to the very nail holes and the giving up of the Ghost. This latter was also the stopping point for much of the art in the devotional tradition of the West during the Middle Ages, a tradition the foremost exponent of which was perhaps Mathias Grünewald. The Crucifixion is a symbol of pain and of the utter solitude in which it is borne. But Christian Universality says: this is the Destiny of Man. But it is not the end, it is a path.

The Russian ikon tradition is seeped in a clarity and calm which specifically proclaims continuity beyond the Crucifixion. In the same way as its Byzantine forerunners, it bears witness to the heavenly union of the spirit and its liberation from the flesh in the Passion.

But this is not Neizvestny's theme. Ever conscious of the mystery of death and the hereafter, and with a memento of death etched into his body with deep scars, he

194

cannot but experience with even greater intensity the intimate concomitancy of the spirit with the body and all other things this side of the grave.

His theme is assuredly the fusion of contrasts here and now, rather than their isolation. This is how this spiritualistic Dionysian figure identifies himself with the world.

But since the way of things, also according to his view, is such that the exalted is to be found again in the humble, and both are reflections of each other as heaven in a raindrop, divine love in the erotic, and the Creation in Man, it is perhaps possible to discern a theme in Neizvestny's art other than that which is immediately apparent. Through his work runs a rhythmic current of vitality. Should we seek comparisons, our thoughts lead us in the direction of such "heathen" manifestations as Viking ornamentation, Scythian art, Aztec sculpture, Hellenic art and Picasso.

A Christian revival such as many have nevertheless seen in Neizvestny's art, presupposes, as in all revivals, that the instigator has gone back to, and identified himself with, the Beginning, even if he does not come to remain there.

In this context, it means going back to the spiritual beliefs such as they existed wherever the impulse from Jesus Christ manifested itself, and such as they were repeated both in individuals and in societies down through history right until the de-Christianised, atomised present state of the World in both East and West.

This is the stuff that blood and suffering are made of and of which Neizvestny is a part, though mind you, he is still conscious of a "vertical" timelessness. This latter is of decisive significance.

He lives to build a temple to this age of transition in which it can see its inner state. Those who give him the opportunity to do this, may help to redeem it.

ERNST NEIZVESTNY – BIOGRAPHICAL NOTES

1926   Born in Sverdlovsk in the Ural Mountains.

1942–45   Served as a volunteer in the Red Army. Severely wounded in Austria in April 1945.

1946   Starts to study art and philosophy in Riga.

1947–54   Student at the Surikov Institute in Moscow. At the same time studies philosophy at Moscow University.

1955   Becomes a member of the Union of Soviet Artists.

1957   Wins two medals at the International Festival of Youth in Moscow.

1958   Starts work on his «Gigantomachia» series. Develops his «Heart of Man» into «The Tree of Life».

1962   Participates at a showing in the Manège in Moscow and becomes involved in an argument with Khrushchev.

1965   Exhibits at the Museum of Modern Art in Belgrade, and, together with Marc Chagall, at the Grosvenor Gallery in London.

1966   Exhibits at the Museum of Modern Art in Vienna and the Galérie Lambert in Paris.

1969   Shows his illustrations for Dante's Inferno at the Galleri Astley in Köping, Sweden. Wins an international competition for the decoration of the Aswan Dam in Egypt. This is completed in 1971.

1970   Exhibits at the Musée d'Art Moderne de la Ville de Paris and the Museo Belle Arti in Locarno.

1972   Exhibits at the Museum of Modern Art in Tel Aviv.

1974   Executes the tombstone for Nikita Khrushchev. Takes part in the exhibition «Progressive currents in Moscow» at the Bochum Museum in W. Germany.

1975   Shows in Vienna, Berlin and at the Lincoln Center, New York.

1976   Emigrates to the West and settles in Zurich. Exhibits at the Stedelijk Museum in Amsterdam and at the Kunstverein in Constance in W. Germany.

1977   Moves to New York but keeps his studio in Zurich. Shows at the Galérie Scheidegger in Zurich, the Galleri Astley in Uttersberg, Sweden and the Städtisches Museum in Leverkusen, W. Germany. Starts lecturing on art and philosophy at universities in the USA.

1978   Shows at the Thielska Galleriet in Stockholm, the Lilla Galleriet in Umeå, Sweden, the Menzoni Galleria d'Arte in Milan and the Centro d'Arte Dolomiti in Cortina.

1979   Shows at Eduard Nakhamkin Fine Art in New York and at other galleries.

1981   Shows for the first time in Norway at Holst Halvorsens Kunsthandel in Oslo.

1984   Shows at the Magna Gallery in San Francisco. Work is started on the "Tree of Life" Museum in Uttersberg, Sweden.

The following is a selection of the museums and public places in which Neizvestny's work is represented:

Moderna Museet, Stockholm
Museum of Modern Art, New York
Kennedy Center, Washington D.C.
The Jewish Museum, New York
Sculpture Park, Schulman Building, New York
Musée d'Art Moderne, Paris
Vatican Museum of Modern Ecclesiastical Art.
Sven-Olov Andersons Torg, Köping, Sweden.
Värdshuset Flottaren, Vansbro, Sweden.
The Municipality of Oslo Art Collection.